Chakra Healing for Beginners

Balance Chakra Frequencies, Remove
Blockage, Increase Flow of Life Force
Energy, and Maintain Harmonic
Resonance

Erin Hanson

Table of Contents

Introduction

The flowers inside your body are more beautiful than the flowers outside—full of fragrance and love. They are the sunshine and the medicine of your soul. Oh lost one, come back to the soul, you'll be happier than ever before. —Amit Ray

Complementary and Alternative Medicine (CAM) has climbed popularity rankings in countries like the USA, UK, and Australia, with people diverting from conventional medicine to find holistic healing. In the USA, reports show that more than 21% of the population has accepted CAM despite there being distrust and skepticism, especially among medical professionals (Phutrakool, 2022).

After trying different procedures and medications that don't work, people often look for other options. When we want to know more about something, we find ourselves typing in a few keywords on a search engine. Sounds simple and effective. Yet is it? There's way too much information out there, and it can be extremely confusing. The moment you start to believe in the content of one website, another will pop up and try to convince you otherwise. Have you gone through this tiring drill while trying to find useful advice about chakra healing? Don't worry, you're not the only one.

Testimonies from celebrities, thousands of videos, and the large number of books written on the subject have made enough people curious about chakra healing. You might have found the basic idea sketched out somewhere, but still don't really know how to use the chakras to ensure general wellness. As beginners, it isn't easy to navigate through the vast array of information and find what's relevant. Then there are coaches who offer their services at a cost that not everyone can afford. So, what's needed at this point? You require a curated guide to chakra healing, something that has answers to all your questions, and you can always return to it if you feel lost while on your journey. I was in the same situation when I started out; I didn't know where to look. Now that I've done extensive research and practiced these healing techniques myself, I thought it'd be great if I could share my knowledge and experiences with others.

Since I've been through a lot of turmoil before I started to benefit from chakra healing, I understand where you're at and how you feel. I realize how frustrating it can be when you keep trying all sorts of strategies to get better, but none of them seem to have the desired effect on your body and mind. When you first learned about the possibilities that Chakra healing can open up for you, I'm sure you must have had an ecstatic moment before you felt you're being buried under a load of content. I can relate to this feeling, but let me assure you that you've arrived at the right place. This book will open up the world of possibilities but also provide you with the tools you'll need to explore this new world.

The first question you might have about the chakras is perhaps how they can help you. I'll explain the concept as we progress, but here's a quick look at the benefits of harnessing the power of the chakras.

You'll achieve balance through meditation. The seven chakras are essentially awareness points. When you focus on each of them, you gain a new kind of awareness. Love, security, power, insight, and clarity are some qualities you can develop by improving focus on the chakras.

Sometimes considered gateways, the chakras enable energy to enter your mind and body. When not utilized to the fullest potential, this energy remains inert. Concentrating on the chakras will help you make use of this energy to grow stronger—physically, mentally, and emotionally.

Overall wellness is the main goal of chakra healing. Ancient yogic practices sought to unite the body with the universe as life force met spirituality. The life force moves upward from the root chakra and meets the spiritual vitality of the seventh chakra to create harmony.

Celia Fernandez, a lifestyle writer at Oprahmag.com, writes how her life transformed after she had her aura cleansed. She had been dealing with stress and recent changes in her life made it hard for her to cope with the pressure of her new job. To add to that, her father's failing health resulted in a tense situation at home. While she was never one to express her emotions, when her friend suggested she should see a healer, she agreed. After getting her aura and chakras cleansed, she felt like a weight had been removed (Fernandez, 2018).

We're all surrounded by negative energy in some form or the other. At the same time, we have the power to invite positivity into our lives. All it takes is a clear understanding of this power. This book will help you gain a new perspective on life by introducing you to the seven chakras and their potential. Imagine how it would feel when your worries melt away, allowing you to enjoy every moment. You've been waiting so long to heal from the stress and illnesses that are barring you from living happily. Through my experiences, I've learned that I have strength within me; all I need to be happy is to unleash my true capability. Now you can do the same.

Without guidance, it's hard to truly benefit from chakra healing. I had to struggle to find sources that would point me in the right direction. Many people make the mistake of watching a couple of videos and jumping right in, thinking a few meditation sessions are all you need. The problem with this is, no matter how good the meditations are, unless you're aware of what each chakra stands for, you can't quite make sense of anything. To help you understand better, I've included the history and philosophies behind chakra healing before going into elaborate explanations of each chakra. Toward the end of the book, I've also provided scientific studies that back this practice. Of course, there are some rituals for you to get started. When you're on the last page, I'm sure you will have learned how to unlock the healing potential of the chakras and live a peaceful, harmonious life.

Chapter 1:

The Chakra System

Chakra is a Sanskrit word meaning "disk" or "wheel" situated at certain points in your body that can be referred to as energy centers. These "disks" are associated with nerve bundles and major organs (Sullivan, 2020). Part of a system of meditative and esoteric processes known as Tantra, the chakras are present in both Hindu and Buddhist spiritual practices. Ancient texts don't agree on the number of chakras; while Buddhist texts allude to five points of focus, ancient Hindu scriptures mention six of seven "pranas" or energy centers which later came to be regarded as chakras.

It was only in the 20th century that western scholars and spiritualists began to look into the philosophy of the chakras. Their interpretation has become the basis of current perspectives on the subject. Even the rainbow colors associated with the chakras are a modern concept. Chakras have influenced the way we look at crystals and minerals, shaping alternative healing practices. Astrological signs and tarot cards also take inspiration from the chakra system. In short, many elements of the New Age movement are linked to meditative chakra healing practices.

The Hindu concept of a physical body and subtle body helps in understanding the chakra system. While the physical body is visible to us, the subtle body consists of the mind and emotions. Both factors complement each other—one has a notable impact on the other. Any problem with the subtle body can affect your health in a negative way. Similarly, health issues can disrupt the smooth workings of the subtle body. Keeping the chakras in alignment essentially suggests healing the subtle body for your wellness.

Typically, the chakras are thought to be along the spinal column, from your head to the base of your spine. We consider the importance of seven main energy points, but traditions have always varied. For better understanding and healing purposes, we'll learn about the seven principal chakras in this book. However, I'll be introducing you to the concept of 114 chakras a little later in the chapter.

What's Held in a Chakra?

A chakra contains emotions, memories, actions, and experiences. Specific chakras relate to particular feelings and actions, but each has to be aligned for your well-being. The question that you might be asking now is, how does this whole system work? It's a vortex of several types of energies—some good, but the others not so much. Think of it as a friend's circle. You'd want kind, caring, and fun people to be in it, not the jealous or arrogant ones. Similarly, you'd want to assist the flow of positive energies into the chakras and remove negative energies that are stopping you from living a better life. These negative energies block the path through which positive energies are supposed to enter. Once a chakra is blocked, a part of your life will be affected. That's when you need to take steps to remove the blockage.

Chakra and Health

An analogy provided by Sri Sri Ravishankar explains how chakras are related to health or why they are important for our wellness (Neumann, 2022). According to him, there are rivers of energy flowing into the body as well as out from it. Chakras act as intersections for these rivers. Naturally, if one of the chakras is blocked, the river will not flow in the right direction. Your health will thus be negatively affected.

Damla Aketin, founder of A Drop of Om, says that the chakras regulate the distribution of energies through your body (Neumann,

2022). Imagine you're injured and instead of applying first aid to the wound, the doctor treats some other part of your body that didn't sustain any injuries. Would you heal? Of course not. Use the same logic here—the chakras ensure positive energies don't flow past the area in need of healing. Every chakra is linked to the organs or nerve bundles, but keep in mind, their role isn't limited to improving physical health.

What Is a Blocked Chakra

For the body to work well, the chakras need to be coordinated and function as a system. If one is not balanced, the others might soon lose their alignment. You could be wondering why the chakras fall out of alignment and the answer to that is there are several possible scenarios. The most common scenario is a traumatic event or a serious illness that affects one of the chakras. Just like your cortisol level shoots up when you're anxious, the body kicks into flight or fight mode to fix the problem in the affected chakra. As a result, the other chakras don't receive enough energy. Once the energy flow stops, the chakra will be blocked, and this will compromise your health.

In this context, it's important to note how physical symptoms and emotional responses are interlinked. Let's say your sacral chakra (located near the abdomen) is not balanced. You might experience aches and discomfort in the abdominal region. Due to the physical pain, you'll most likely entertain negative emotions. Now let's consider the opposite. Suppose you aren't emotionally stable because of a recent tragedy. Grief and hopelessness can cause problems that will manifest as physical illnesses.

Importance of Chakras

You've learned about the chakras and the whole process that makes sure energies or life forces enter the centers located in your body. Here's a brief list of the most relevant points.

- The chakras control the flow of energy to various parts of the body. As any excess or lack can cause issues with your health, regulation is necessary.

- Acting as centers of stored emotions, the chakras have the power to release or hold back feelings. Hence, if they are not working as they should, your emotions could be stuck.

- Mental health can suffer greatly due to imbalances in your chakras. The direction of energy flow determines how your brain will react to circumstances, so there's a chance you'd be overwhelmed if the seven chakras are not in alignment.

- No matter what you do to cure your illnesses or just feel better in general, the chakras need to be aligned for you to heal fully.

Balancing Your Chakras

In the chapters that follow, I'll be giving you tips to balance the chakras and maintain a healthy flow of energies. I know that some people have a false idea about this topic—they think it's not possible to practice chakra healing without incorporating difficult yoga postures or prolonged meditations into their daily routine. Here's a little secret— you can heal even if you're not a pro at yoga and meditation. I'll tell you how you can do it but first things first, note what chakra healing does to your life! For that extra kick of motivation, below are some of the positive effects of balancing your chakras.

You won't be too stressed out by your surroundings, even if it's a disturbing situation. Keeping your chakras in alignment gives you the power to handle difficulties and overcome stress.

You'll find a new purpose in life. At this point, you might not be thrilled with the prospects life has to offer; you could be considering your future and sulking. Once the energy in your body is correctly distributed, you won't be feeling this way.

The moment you have a purpose, you'll be working towards your goals in a more methodical way. There won't be any disarray or ambiguity.

You'll realize your inner godliness, which will help you connect to the spiritual realm. Understanding the spiritual world not only helps you be calm in times of chaos, but it also helps you be grateful for the things you have and release resentment or other negative emotions.

Cultivating psychic powers becomes easier when your chakras are balanced. You'll succeed in making intuitive decisions based on what's best for you in the long run.

Colors and Chakras

Do an image search of the chakras and you'll immediately be looking at pictures with vibrant colors. Although they might tempt you to think it's all advertising, the truth is far removed from that. Each chakra is associated with a specific color and to maximize the benefits of healing, you'll need to use these colors in various rituals. Don't be discouraged by thinking the rituals are too elaborate; they are quite the opposite. However, colors play a significant role.

I can imagine what you're going to ask next—you aren't sure why energy centers should be represented by colors. Well, the simple answer is that colors have different vibration frequencies, as do the chakras. Using the right color for the chakra's frequency activates the full potential of the chakra. Christopher Hill, an English writer and philosopher, introduced the idea of associating each chakra with one of the seven colors of the rainbow. When light passes through a prism, the colors formed as a result have different wavelengths. Matching their wavelength to the vibration pattern of the chakras helped determine which chakra would be attributed to what color.

Why is this important for your health? Any changes in the vibration of a chakra will either attract too much or too little energy toward it. The right color will rectify this imbalance. You'll also start to think optimistically about healing and recovery. Yes, colors are incredibly powerful and chakra healing practices use their potential for holistic healing.

The Seven Chakras

Despite the presence of more energy centers in our body and ancient belief systems that claimed the existence of more than seven chakras, we have narrowed it down to seven because these seven chakras have the greatest impact. Here's a quick look at them.

Root Chakra (Muladhara): Located at the base of the spine and is symbolic of grounding, confidence, and balance.

Sacral Chakra (Svadhisthana): Located near the lower abdomen and represents sexuality, creativity, and emotional wellness.

Solar Plexus Chakra (Manipura): Located near the upper abdomen and represents self-esteem and confidence.

Heart Chakra (Anahata): Located near the heart and symbolizes that connection between matter and spirit.

Throat Chakra (Visuddha): Located near the throat and stands for communicative abilities.

Third-Eye Chakra (Ajna): Located on the forehead and relates to psychic or spiritual powers.

Crown Chakra (Sahasrara): Located at the top of the head and regulates intelligence, awareness, beauty, and spiritual connection.

The 114 Chakras

Even though we aren't going to learn about each of the 114 chakras in this book, additional knowledge about them will strengthen your concept of the seven chakras. The oral traditions mention the existence of 114 chakras in the body that connect with each other to form a map of energy flow. Dr. Amit Ray followed this tradition as he believed balancing energies in these chakras will ensure complete healing (Zeeshan, 2022).

72,000 channels of energy or "Nadis" flow to and from the 114 chakras. The Nadis are not just part of our physical bodies, they are also present in our astral bodies. Being channels of life energy or prana, they act as a network. According to Dr Amit Ray, the Nadis can be divided into three broad categories—collection point, purification facilities, and distribution network. Our senses are the collection points from where energy is transferred to the purification centers. Glands and organs constitute the purification facilities that analyze the type of energies and relay the information to the distribution channels. Various parts of the body—muscles, joints, ligaments, veins, and arteries—aid the process (Ray, 2017).

Names and definitions of these chakras have been interpreted differently, so we don't have exact terms for them. Some scholars and yogis prefer a 12-chakra system where earth, universe, galactic, and divine are five chakras included with the seven. If we are to consider Dr. Amit Ray's version, the 114 chakras are divided into seven major, 21 minor, and 86 micro chakras. Generally, this system isn't starkly different because the seven major chakras make the foundational element. One crucial distinguishing factor is the role of the minor chakras.

Minor Chakras

These chakras are located near the primary energy centers. They hardly work independently, as their job is to support the seven major chakras. By preventing toxins, boosting immunity, and improving reproductive health the minor chakras complement the efforts of the major chakras. You'll find them in the following places:

- in both ears

- Above each breast

- At the intersection of the clavicle

- On each palm of your hand

- On each sole of your feet

- Above each eye

- In your reproductive organs

- In your liver

- In your stomach

- In your spleen

- Behind each knee

- In your thymus gland

- Near your Solar Plexus Chakra

Kundalini

You might have heard this term because it's often used to denote a form of potent energy that can enhance your abilities. Broadly speaking, Kundalini refers to the energy at the base of the spine or the area where your root chakra is located. It's depicted as a serpent resting in a coiled position. Most of this energy isn't used in daily life but if you practice Kundalini yoga and meditation, when done correctly, can take you one step closer to enlightenment. But your chakras must be aligned, and you should have already achieved healing before you venture to practice Kundalini yoga.

Bhavsagar

Bhavsagar, or the void, is the "unenlightened awareness" within us. You have the potential for enlightenment because this awareness is within every one of us. Through spiritual practice and meditation, you can fill this void. Don't worry, it's not as intimidating as it might sound. That space may be empty now, but as you continue your spiritual journey, you'll get closer to filling it. In fact, you can start now! Eliminate negative thoughts and discourage pessimistic visions; you'll get a head start on the journey already.

Key Takeaways

You are not far from the healing you're seeking right now. Read the following key points and you'll realize how much you've learned so far. I also have a reflective exercise for you. Think about the chakras and the energy flowing through your body. Ask yourself if you feel there's a problem in the distribution of energies. Your answer will help you figure out where the imbalances are.

- The chakras are the main energy centers in your body. They regulate the flow of energy and affect your general health.

- Although philosophies and scholarship differ in their outlook, modern western yogis have accepted the existence of seven chakras.

- Located along the spinal column, these seven chakras usually concern themselves with the organs nearest to their position.

- A network of "Nadis" or channels distribute energies from one point to another. Together, the Nadis and chakras form a network.

- Each of us has the potential to find enlightenment because we have energy stored inside us and an awareness that can be cultivated.

With basic knowledge of the chakra system comes the urge to know more about its history. You are probably wondering who first discovered this complex network inside us and how they stumbled upon this idea. So, let's dig a little deeper to find out!

Chapter 2:

The Seven Chakras

You might have guessed from the content in the previous chapter that this one's going to be about the ancient origins of the chakra system. Yes, the seven-chakra network is a fairly modern concept, but it is rooted in ancient oral traditions. The Vedas (1500 to 500 BCE) mention the existence of chakras. In the Cudamini Upanishad, Yoga-Shikkha, and Shandilya Upanishad, a word roughly spelled as "Cakra" has been used extensively. New-Age author Anodea Judith has expanded on the ancient concepts to explain the chakra system and its meaning from a modern western perspective.

Chakra Science and Philosophy

The Vedas contain the essence of Indian philosophy. If we read the Vedas, we understand the worldview of ancient philosophers. Their true wisdom is also manifested in the scientific formulation of the chakra system. Two opposite forces unite to create life. In biology, we call this the union of the male and female counterparts of a species. Ancient philosophers thought of the same concept (Schneider, 2019). Shiva and Shakti are the two opposite forces—while Shiva represents the supreme consciousness, Shakti is life-giving energy deified as the mother goddess. The physical body is intertwined with the spirit, and neither can exist alone.

What do Ancient Texts Say?

I introduced this chapter with a reference to the Upanishads. To add to that, it's important to note that the Yoga Upanishads were the first to mention chakras as psychic centers of consciousness (Schneider, 2019). Interestingly, the yoga Upanishads were also the first to delineate meditation principles. Chakras were the centers to focus on while meditating. Concentration establishes a connection with the energy stored in the area of focus. Western scholars later developed the seven-chakra system from the idea of psychic centers. Arthur Avalon, who wrote The Serpent Power (1911) took inspiration from three other sources apart from the Upanishads—Sat-Chakra Nirupana (1577), Paduka Panchaka (10th Century), and the Goraksha Satakam (10th Century). Mostly known for their meditation techniques, these books provide the foundation for chakra healing practices.

Significance of the 114 Chakras

While we're on the topic of meditation, it's necessary to revisit the 114 chakra map that you read about in the previous chapter. Dr. Amit Ray expanded on the seven chakras and came up with a theory that takes into account the impact of every kind of energy. Ray scientifically connects the chakras with glands, hormones, brain areas, neurons, neurotransmitters, brain-gut, and the Hypothalamic-Pituitary-Adrenal (HPA) axis (Schneider, 2019). The seven-chakra system is also designed to correspond to different parts of the body; however, the plurality of energy points helps you concentrate on specifics while meditating. I think it's best to first attempt healing through the seven-chakra process and then proceed to delve into the science behind these 114 chakras.

Neuropsychology of the Chakras

Since the chakras are associated with organs, glands, and nerve centers, they directly relate to the physical and psychological state of a person. Your abilities are determined by the levels of energy in your chakras. Unlike other philosophies, the chakra system places the significance of energy over everything else. You always have the capacity to improve your health and wellness; it all depends on how you retain balance in the chakras.

Let's compare the chakras to neurotransmitters because this analogy clears doubts regarding the scientific foundation of the chakra healing process. GABA and Glutamate, two neurotransmitters with opposite functions, act as complements. If the brain has glutamate alone, it would always be excited. On the other hand, if it's dominated by GABA, it wouldn't be capable of performing complicated activities. Now, how can we draw a similarity between the neurotransmitters and the chakra system? When out of balance, the energy levels suppress certain kinds of activities to prioritize others.

Chakra Macrocosm and Microcosm

Physics operates on both the micro and macro levels. Relativity or physics of the extremely large constitute the macrocosm whereas quantum mechanics or physics of the extremely small form the microcosm. In chakra theory, Shiva and Shakti (the macrocosm and the microcosm) are always united by fire and heat. Dr. Amit Ray suggests that the inner world and the outer world are inherently connected and disturbances in one can lead to chaos in the other. The principles of polarity are just as applicable to you as they are to the universe at large. Suppose there's an imbalance of energies in the outer world. It will result in catastrophes such as floods and droughts. Similarly, energy imbalance in your body will lead to illnesses and psychological problems.

Chakra Philosophy

I have briefly discussed the concept of subtle bodies and how the chakras are subtle bodies working in unison with your physical body.

According to ancient Indian philosophy, five elements that make the universe also shape and mold the human body. These five elements are air (vayu), space (akasha), water (jal), fire (agni), and earth (prithvi). We have subtle bodies or nonphysical bodies governed by prana or life force. Every thought you have is part of the subtle body. Thoughts and emotions are distributed through the network of Nadis and reach the energy centers. Not all of these thoughts materialize as actions. Some remain in our subtle bodies, affecting the way we feel.

Why the Chakra Servers Shouldn't Be Down

Vedic educator Michelle Fondin uses a brilliant example to show why the chakra network must be superfast. You wouldn't want to wait for an hour to search something on the internet (Fondin, 2018)! Imagine the frustration you feel when your Wi-Fi is down, and you absolutely need a piece of information that's crucial for your work project. Your body feels the same frustration when it takes ages for information to reach its particular destination. Blocked energy centers cause extreme disarray and halt the easy flow of communication between mind and body. Remember how the senses receive energy from the world outside and send it along the network of Nadis? If the major recipients of energy or the seven main chakras are blocked, it won't be possible for each organ or neuron to be aware of what's going on.

The Ultimate Goal

I'm sure you've landed on websites and articles that talk about self-realization as the ultimate goal of yogic practice. Without sufficient background knowledge, you won't be able to understand the meaning of self-realization. Tantra, Ayurveda, and Yoga are on the same page regarding the quest for the realization of the Self. Purusha or the pure universal consciousness is not tangible. It has no form, but it creates form or prakruty. While prakruty is changeable, its creator remains unchanged. All life on earth falls under the large banner of prakruty, be it the natural world or human existence. As you are now part of prakruty, your goal is to reach the purusha or universal consciousness. Through meditation, you can indeed achieve this goal, and aligning your chakras is the first step. The Yogic sutras of Patanjali elaborate on how you can overcome the physical self to connect with the universal spirit.

Gunas

Gunas are qualities that are embedded in our prakruti from the time of birth. They are your connection to the Purusha. You will need each of them for various reasons. Divided into three categories, the gunas provide you with the ability to utilize all your resources.

- Sattva: This is the quality of peacefulness, purity, and alertness.

- Rajas: This is an active energy required to meet your targets.

- Tamas: The spirit of darkness, this quality helps you sleep and rest.

We need the three gunas for our well-being. They are not put to use simultaneously but are rather applicable to widely differing circumstances.

Doshas

We have a unique mind-body makeup consisting of our doshas. To complement the three gunas, we have three doshas—Vata, Pitta, and Kalpa. Our gunas and doshas make us who we are and shape the course of our lives. But the trick is to go beyond these individual malleable traits to reach the unchanging universe. One way you can do it is to start your chakra healing journey. Keeping your energies in balance is a necessary step towards self-realization. When your chakras are aligned, you have optimal energy levels. You should let your body reap the benefits of the physical world but not in excess. Gradually, you'll attain freedom from the gunas and doshas that tie you to the created world and move closer to the universal consciousness. Self-realization is another term for moksha or liberation—the enlightened state achieved after your ties to the surrounding world are obliterated.

Key Takeaways

We should always try to know as much as possible about the origin and history of philosophical thought. It's only then that we'll comprehend why this thought is good for us. Here's a brief recap of the history of the chakra system:

- Vedic texts dating back to 1500 BCE refer to the chakras, but the concept was developed for yogic and meditative practices.

- The chakra system is rooted in science. Your brain has two main types of neurotransmitters, and they work together so we can perform a range of activities. The chakras hold and channel energies that ensure wellness by maintaining perfect balance.

- Purusha or universal consciousness is responsible for the creation of prakruti or the tangible world around us, including ourselves.

- Gunas and doshas, individual traits and qualities, can be overcome to reach a higher level of consciousness, but they'd need to be balanced in the first place.

Now that you've grasped the basic framework of the chakra system, it's time for a detailed analysis of their separate roles.

Chapter 3:

Root Chakra—Muladhara

Let's begin a deeper analysis of the seven main chakras with Muladhara or the root chakra. When we meditate, we begin by focusing on the root chakra because it acts as a foundation for overall wellness and spiritual upliftment. It's important to be grounded if we want to improve the quality of life we're living. Think of finding a cure to any illness—the first step is to always understand the causes which lie at the bottom of it. Chakra healing is a process that takes into consideration all the problems acting as a roadblock to your general well-being. To remove this roadblock or get past it, you must understand why it's there in the first place. Maybe there's a physical ailment limiting your ability to enjoy good health. Unless you find out what's wrong, there's no way you can proceed toward what's right.

Location

The root chakra or the Muladhara is situated at the base of the spine.

Color

Red is the designated color for this chakra.

Meaning

Essentially, the root chakra symbolizes grounding. In doing so, however, it entails physical identity and mindset. Your foundation determines stability or the lack of it. To build a strong foundation, you have to concentrate on the muladhara.

Mantra

LAM—the first chant you'll hear when you start meditating. Meaning "I can't grow from an unsteady foundation", this mantra helps you be more determined about creating a sturdy base for your goals.

Element

Earth is the element connected to muladhara because we are rooted to the earth in the first place. To strengthen our foundation, we should connect with the earth.

A Brief Overview of Muladhara

People have a habit of highly regarding what's at the helm, discarding the importance of what's at the base. This psychology comes into play when some people dismiss the muladhara chakra as the lowest chakra. Being the foundation of life, it is of supreme essence and can never be downplayed. We need only to think of a developing fetus to understand the role that energy plays in shaping our lives. For the physical body to form, the energy mechanism or Pranmaya Kosha has to be right. Any irregularity will result in abnormalities or anomalies in the physical body.

Yoga poses often rely on the muladhara chakra because, without a firm base, the pose might be distorted. Reflect on how a child first learns to walk. The process starts with crawling, then standing up, and finally walking. If the baby doesn't learn how to stand up first, how will they walk? Similarly, when the same logic is applied to the muladhara chakra, you'll realize that ignoring it would lead to chaos in the energy flow inside your body, creating major imbalances that could threaten your health and well-being.

Kayakalpa Yoga and Muladhara

Among the yogic practices that focus on the muladhara chakra, kayakalpa is the foremost. Kaya refers to the body and kalpa denotes a long period of time. When clubbed together, these two words indicate "a long life". This school of yoga stresses the need to stabilize bodily functions, so they don't deteriorate quickly. To put it differently, it's slowing down the process of aging and prolonging life. Even if you don't follow the principles of kayakalpa yoga, you can use this concept to get healthier and mitigate the effects of aging on your body and mind.

Imbalances in the Root Chakra

Since the root chakra is responsible for stability, imbalances can cause severe health hazards. Psychological problems like anxiety and paranoia might develop as a result of this. You could also experience physical illnesses related to the colon, bladder, or lower body in general.

Reason for Imbalance

It's believed that the struggles of our ancestors and the hardships they had to endure are manifested in our lives through imbalances in the root chakra. As it's the place where ancestral memories of difficult times are embedded, we go through situations when we feel hopeless and distraught. Of course, this doesn't happen suddenly or without ground. Our own experiences and the circumstances we are in contribute to these imbalances. For example, let's suppose someone has been ill for a considerable amount of time. Things are running amok for them even as they recover. Since their body and mind aren't in the best shape, the root chakra turns into a space for negative emotions.

Symptoms of Root Chakra Imbalance

How would you know that everything is not right with you due to root chakra imbalance? At times we don't feel good but can't quite understand why. If you are experiencing any of the following symptoms, you might need to work towards building a better foundation for your health through the stabilization of the root chakra.

Lower Body Aches

Since the root chakra is associated with the lower body, occasional pains suggest there could be an imbalance. Maybe you've tried medicines and exercises to heal the persistent aches but nothing's doing the trick. Perhaps it's time you looked at chakra healing.

Depression and Anger

When you're not standing on firm ground, it's only natural you'll feel frustrated about your condition. Without any improvement in the state of things, you can become depressed. Another aspect of root chakra imbalance is a constant feeling of anger and resentment.

Listlessness

Another typical feeling related to root chakra imbalance is the lack of desire to do anything. You'd want to simply lie down and do nothing for a long period of time. Usually, someone going through this doesn't want to work or engage in any leisure activities. They are unable to find joy in anything, so after a while, they quit trying.

No Sense of Belonging

Although it doesn't happen in every case of root chakra imbalance, some people tend to think they don't belong anywhere. Their attempt to seek friends with whom they'd be able to connect often meets with disappointment. Loneliness gradually leads to depression.

Removing the Blockages

You have the power to re-establish the balance that will help you get back on track. First, you need to find ways to remove the blockages that are disturbing the root chakra and not letting it remain in a state of harmony.

Opening the Root Chakra

Here are some ways in which you can open the muladhara chakra and bring back the right balance.

Incense and Essential Oils

Smells can have a healing effect on your body and mind. While some fragrances help you be calm, some others might fill you up with positive energy. Remember though that it's important to distinguish the aromas and understand what role they play in chakra healing. For root chakra balancing, you can use the following:

- Earthy essential oils like ajwain, black seed, black spruce, buddha wood, cardamom, cassia bark, cedarwood

- Candles

- Incenses like sandalwood, cedarwood, rosewood, cypress

- Cloves, black pepper, ginger

Affirmations

Spelling out your intentions and voicing your goals are a major part of creating new habits while releasing emotions that are stuck in your mind. List a few affirmations that relate to the root chakra and repeat it every day, preferably in the morning. To balance your root chakra, you should focus on your foundation, home, stability, and safety. Below are some examples but you can list your unique intentions.

- The universe has everything that I need

- I don't have to worry because I'm safe

- I am healthy and I care for my body

- My home is a happy place for me

- My finances are stable

Postures for Stability

Yoga postures or asanas help you become more spiritually aware. For the root chakra, asanas you practice must have a connection with the earth or the foundation. Some asanas that work best for this purpose include—child's pose, warrior pose, mountain, and squat.

Mindful Walking and Other Ways of Connecting With the Earth

Your goal is to connect with nature but not everyone is comfortable with practicing mindfulness or meditation while sitting in the same position for a considerable amount of time. An alternative to this is going on a nature trail or being aware of your natural surroundings while walking. You'll need to pay attention to your breathing and the steps you take. Think about walking towards your true home while noticing what's familiar. Nature is always ready to welcome you with open arms, you just need to decide to spend more time in its company. Be outdoors more often, meet your friends in a park instead of some closed space, walk on the beach, go wandering in the woods—you'll feel your bonding with the earth get stronger!

Healing From Insecurities

Past insecurities, particularly those developed in childhood, can keep you from feeling safe in your current environment. Of course, healing won't be a quick process. It starts with recognizing the insecurities and understanding why you have them in the first place. Don't lose hope if it takes more time than you'd imagined. Eventually, you will heal, and your root chakra will open up, bringing in safety and stability.

Asanas to Open and Align Muladhara

As mentioned earlier, asanas help your body get in tune with spiritual forces, empowering you to clear blockages. Yoga poses that you should practice regularly to open the root chakra and remove imbalances are:

- Pavanamuktasana (knee to chest pose)

- Janu Sirsansana (head to knee pose)

- Padmasana (lotus flexion)

- Malasana (squatting pose)

In Balance, Too Much, or Not Enough?

Imbalance does not always mean there's a lack of root chakra energy. People often make the mistake of thinking that they don't have enough of the energy that improves chakral balance, but it's important to first understand why things aren't as they should be. Maybe you believe your root chakra isn't balanced but the problem could be lying elsewhere. Don't worry though, you can figure out if your chakra is in balance or otherwise. Here's a brief guide to help you.

Is the Root Chakra In Balance?

Balanced root chakra would mean you're grounded and stable. So, ask yourself the following questions:

Am I confident about myself?

If your answer is "yes", the possibility of your root chakra being balanced is quite high. Confidence comes from grounding and acceptance of your reality.

Do I believe I am capable of committing to my duties?

When you think you're not capable, it implies that you've either taken on too much or you're not on the right path. Suppose you are working a job that doesn't suit you. You'll always be uncomfortable and dissatisfied. In this situation, you'll be more likely to experience anxiety and depression. A positive response to this question, however, would suggest balance in the root chakra.

How would I describe my relationship with my family, friends, and work?

A sense of disconnect for loved ones is a sign of imbalance in the root chakra. You'll feel as if you can't interact with anyone without getting into unnecessary arguments or that you can't find happiness because you're emotionally distant from everyone else.

Too Much

Sometimes, the energy might be beyond the levels of requirement, which creates an imbalance. Below are some signs that you have excess energy in the root chakra.

Greed: You want more of everything, be it money, fame, or attention from loved ones. When you can't have what you want, you feel disgruntled. This doesn't mean you're an awful person. It could be that you have more energy in the muladhara chakra and therefore are filled with excessive desire.

Arrogance and Pride: Has anyone recently told you that you're behaving rudely or disrespecting other people? You might be surprised to hear this or concerned that you're generally quite kind and humble. Again, when you have a surplus store of energy in your root chakra, you'll tend to behave in ways that aren't characteristic of you. Or even if you have been displaying negative behavior for a long time, it could be because of energy imbalance.

Not Enough

The symptoms of low energy in the root chakra are exactly opposite to the signs discussed in the previous section. Yet, both types are signals making you aware of imbalances in the muladhara. Below are the symptoms you'll notice that are indicative of a lack of energy flow in the root chakra.

You might be doing okay at work, but you still think there's something wrong. No matter how much you do or how hard you try to focus, you're not able to get rid of the dissatisfaction you feel regarding work. Keep in mind that this doesn't have to be a regular job. Suppose you're a stay-at-home parent, you might believe your input is not sufficient or that you're somehow not reaching your potential.

Your loved ones and friends are not as close as they used to be. Although you want to share your thoughts with them and communicate, you're hitting an invisible barrier.

You feel as though you don't know your true self. Remember, this might not be a distinct feeling. One of the prominent fallouts of this is not recognizing what's best for you or failing to find happiness in your everyday life.

How to Boost Energy

After going through the symptoms, if you think you don't have enough energy in the root chakra, do the following:

Wear red clothes and accessories. Red is a color that attracts energy toward the root chakra.

Go on a nature walk barefoot. Taking long walks in the midst of nature is the best way to connect to the earth and find your grounding.

Take care of your physical fitness through activities like gardening, dancing, and exercising (preferably outdoors).

How to Bring Down the Energy Levels

To calm your root energy, follow the steps below:

Remove clutter in your house and do away with items that you don't use any longer. It sounds like a mammoth task but once you get going, it gets easier. Also, you'll have more breathing space!

Get a pedicure! Too much energy might be stored in your lower body, particularly your feet. Cleaning up can be a good way to get rid of excess energy.

Forgive others and yourself. I understand that practicing forgiveness takes time and requires you to change your mindset, but in the end, it's always worth it.

Foods That Help

You can tweak your eating habits a little to channel more energy toward or away from the root chakra. Foods that are red in color, spices, and root vegetables increase root chakra energy. Add them to your diet or remove them to correct the imbalance.

Gems and Crystals

Ideally, red stones and crystals attract root chakra energy. Since it's a bright color, it's easily noticeable and is often used as a warning signal. Being aware of the threats around you helps you remain grounded and since you can prepare to confront these threats, you feel more confident. Apart from red, black is a color that resonates with root chakra energy. Below is a list of stones and crystals that work best for root chakra opening and balance.

Jasper: It's usually red but can also come in orange, black, and blue variants. Known to increase confidence and feel better about yourself, Jasper fosters a better relationship with your reality.

Carnelian: Also mostly red, this stone builds courage and strength to bolster your self-image.

Obsidian: A black stone that is also available in orange, blue, red, and yellow, it provides clarity so you can make better decisions.

Bloodstone: This stone has a dark green body spotted with orange. Mainly noted for providing protection, it also establishes stability in your life.

Tourmaline: Usually black, tourmaline acts as a destroyer of fear. If you're someone who thinks they can't overcome their fear or anxiety, this stone will work for you.

Rhodonite: For people struggling with emotions and wanting to practice forgiveness, Rhodonite is a must-have. Pinkish in color, this stone also supports your body by improving liver and kidney functions.

Garnet: Red is the most common variant of garnet although it's also seen in green, orange, and yellow. It's especially important for stimulating kundalini energy and spiritual upliftment.

Key Takeaways

Now that we're at the end of this chapter, let's take a quick look at what we've learned here:

- The root chakra or muladhara is responsible for providing a solid foundation for your body and soul.

- Too much or too little energy flow in this chakra can cause imbalances that might disrupt your life.

- Greed and arrogance are the most prominent symptoms of excessive muladhara energy.

- Depression, emotional instability, and disconnect from loved ones are signs of low energy in the root chakra.

- Foods that are spicy or red in color aid in balancing the energy and opening up the chakra.

- Red or black gems and crystals are associated with the root chakra.

You now have sufficient knowledge about the muladhara. We'll now be moving upward, and the next chakra is the sacral chakra or Svadhisthana, located a little above the root chakra.

Chapter 4:

Sacral Chakra—Svadhisthana

The second chakra we're going to take a look at is mostly concerned with self-worth, emotions, and desires. Think about a time when you believed you had a lot going on and couldn't make sense of your emotions. It's likely your sacral chakra was out of balance at that point, which is possible when you are undergoing stress or dealing with a particular difficulty. Also known as Svadhisthana, this chakra checks your relationship with emotions, be it your own feelings or that of others. Intrinsically linked to your emotions, desires also have a significant impact on your life. You want to explore your desires and seek pleasure from their fulfillment. The sacral chakra assists in identifying the desires and finding ways to satisfy them. Creativity and sexuality are also fostered by the Svadhisthana.

Introduction to the Sacral Chakra

To gain more understanding of this chakra, let's begin with the basics.

Location

The sacral chakra is located in the lower abdominal area—two inches below the naval and slightly above the pubic bone.

Color

Orange is associated with Svadhisthana, but a lighter form of red is also accepted at times.

Meaning

This chakra nurtures and controls emotions, sexuality, creativity, and pleasure. Of course, these elements are interdependent, but a perfect balance in the energies of the sacral chakra ensures you're not lacking any of them.

Mantra

"Vam" is the mantra chanted for this chakra. It roughly means "I always honor others but not before myself". As the sacral chakra considers self-worth to be essential for happiness, the mantra emphasizes the importance of honoring the self.

Element

Svadhisthana has water as its main element so any ritual aimed to balance energies in this chakra would require the use of water. The fluidity of water alludes to the flexibility of expression and smooth flow of emotions.

An Overview

We've seen how the chakras work together to bring harmony to our lives. Each chakra has a unique role to play, and this is often represented symbolically to help us understand the physical, mental, and spiritual aspects that are enhanced by it. The sacral chakra is symbolized by an orange circle with six lotus petals around it. This symbol has a twofold meaning—the cycle of birth, death, and rebirth as well as the relationship between creativity and the phases of the moon because the circles, when viewed in tangent, appear like a crescent.

You might be curious about the origin of these symbols. Did someone draw them based on the function of each chakra? Well, it's a little deeper than that. Yogis visualized these colors and symbols when they meditated on the powers of the chakras. It's also believed that the vibrations of the seven chakras are reflected through their symbols. Any changes to the design might interfere with the flow of energy and is therefore not recommended.

The Svadhisthana chakra bolsters creativity and sensual enjoyment but as it's not possible to give shape to your desires without knowing what they are, this chakra also improves the perception of your emotions and longings. To be happy and be able to spread happiness, emotional awareness is extremely necessary. Opening up the sacral chakra and maintaining a balance of energies flowing to and from it is a way to be in touch with your feelings and comprehend the expression of other people's emotions. I'll give you an example to make this point clearer. Let's say you're having a bad day. You're angry about everything that went wrong but you can't describe exactly how you're feeling. At this time, your friend rings you up and starts talking about their day, which wasn't the best either. Instead of relating to what they're saying, you become grumpier and more agitated than before. Why is this? The simple answer is, you're not in tune with your emotions and you can't empathize with others who are equally disturbed as you because you aren't able to perceive their situation.

Imbalances in the Sacral Chakra

Blockages in the Svadhisthana chakra can result in several physical, mental, and spiritual problems, depriving us of the ability to thrive and live a happy life. I've divided the symptoms into two main categories below. As you go through them, try to reflect on your health and state of mind, noting down signs of energy blockage in the sacral chakra.

Physical Symptoms

The symptoms listed below concern the general location of the sacral chakra and the physical implications of any anomalies in the region.

- chronic lower back pain

- Urinary Tract Infection (UTI)

- Impotence

- Ovarian cysts

- Reproductive issues

- Pain during intercourse

- Pain in the lower abdomen area

- Illnesses concerning the kidney and bladder

It's important to bear in mind that many of the physical consequences of sacral chakra blockage are exclusive to women. However, if you're a woman thinking it'll be especially difficult for you to control the energy flow to this chakra, let me assure you there's no need to worry. In the upcoming section about the removal of blockages, I'll discuss ways in which women can balance energies in the Svadhisthana chakra for a healthy, fulfilling life.

Mental Health Symptoms

The impact of sacral chakra energy on the mind is equally significant. Here's a glimpse at how you'll feel when the Svadhisthana is out of balance.

- You might feel overwhelmed by emotions or unable to characterize your feelings

- Your sex drive might be excessive, in which case, it's quite common to overindulge in sexual fantasies.

- On the other hand, the sex drive might be lacking, and you won't feel any urge for intimacy.

- Your creativity could be stifled. Irrespective of how creative you used to be, when there's a blockage in the sacral chakra, you'll not retain much of your creative skills.

Why You Need to Align Your Sacral Chakra

Without the sacral chakra in alignment, you will be left with a sense of dissatisfaction no matter what you do. You might make changes in your life to feel better but if there are still imbalances in this chakra, your enjoyment will be tempered by a lingering apprehension of not having all it takes to find pleasure.

Removing the Blockages

Once you've recognized the fact that there's a blockage in your sacral chakra, you should start the healing process. Just as for the root chakra, asanas, meditations, particular colors, gems, and foods will help you open up the Svadhisthana chakra. But let's begin with waking your creative self up through fun activities!

Indulge the Child in You

If you give it sufficient thought, you'll realize that you were much more creative as a child than you are right now. We feel freer to express our creative side at a young age because we are unhindered by opinions and self-criticism. Just imagine the pictures you used to draw and the games you played as children. Now if you're asked to paint a picture or write a poem, you'll hesitate, believing that your efforts will only produce something laughable. You have become self-conscious and wary of appraising eyes. Now if you force yourself, you'll definitely engage in a creative task, but that won't be any good for your sacral chakra.

To be the most creative and direct your energies in the right direction, begin to think like a child. Observe a child at play and you'll realize how they don't bother about anything but the game. You need to cultivate this mentality. No matter what you do to get creative, think of yourself as a child playing their favorite game. Of course, you'll make mistakes and "lose" a few times. Maybe the cake you baked will be a little too sweet or the sketch you make will look a bit odd. Don't blame yourself and abandon your plans to continue pursuing the creative endeavor. It's only the first step; you're expressing your creativity in a unique manner and this counts! Give it some time and you'll see you're enjoying your digs into painting, writing, cooking, singing—whatever piques your interest!

Honor Your Body and Respect Your Feelings

Recognizing your desires and accepting them is a very important part of correcting imbalances in the sacral chakra. The moment you disregard your longings or refuse to explore your emotions, energy will not flow into the Svadhisthana chakra. In most cases, blockages in this chakra result from ignoring feelings or desires. On the other hand, if you're overindulging, you're causing a surplus amount of energy to enter the sacral chakra. As part of your education or beliefs, you might choose to overlook some of your wishes but if your body or mind is paying the price for that, it's time to rethink. Similarly, if you have set no limits for yourself and your emotions are dominating you, you're in need of a change.

Breathwork

Left-nostril breathing is beneficial for the sacral chakra. Place two fingers on your right nostril and use your left nostril to inhale and exhale. Do this ten times and contemplate the mantra "Vam".

Meditation

To meditate on the sacral chakra, focus on the mantra and reflect on your emotions. Listening to music might help the process. You can also meditate outdoors in nature for better concentration.

Asanas

The following asanas are beneficial for removing blockages from the sacral chakra.

Seated Pelvic Circles:

Sit in a half-lotus or cross-legged pose and make circles with your torso. Remember that your hands must be on your knees. Move your torso in one direction about five times and then switch.

Baddha Konasana With Forward Fold:

Also known as the butterfly pose, this asana is good for opening the sacral chakra but particularly helpful for curing lower abdominal problems. While seated, bring your feet together and let your knees fall to the side. Your heels should be close to your pelvis. Once you're in the correct position, fold forward in a way that your torso is lengthened.

Bhujangasana or Cobra Pose:

Lie flat on your stomach and gradually lift your upper body while your navel is still pressed to the ground. Look up or in front of you and take a few deep breaths. For best results, switch to child's pose and stay in that position for thirty seconds before getting up.

In Balance, Too Much, or Not Enough?

To understand whether the energy flow in the sacral chakra is in balance, in excess, or lacking, you should notice your emotions and think about how you feel in terms of contentment. As mentioned previously, the sacral chakra being in balance doesn't mean you'll feel great overall because there could be blockages in other chakras. It's easy to get confused between the symptoms.

In Balance?

Ask yourself the questions listed below to know whether the energy flow to the Svadhisthana is balanced.

Am I feeling too many things at the same time?

If this is a regular occurrence, it would suggest an imbalance. You are probably overwhelmed and unable to discern why you're feeling this way. Mostly, these emotions tend to be negative. However, it's also possible that your positive feelings are tinged with fears and negativity.

Do I know my desires?

You could be repressing your desires and therefore experiencing a lack of fulfillment. When you answer this question with a no and think you're dissatisfied, your sacral chakra is not in alignment.

Do I lack sexual desire or have an excess of it?

Think about your sex life and how you feel about it. As this is a prominent indicator of balance or the lack thereof, reflecting on this question is very important.

Am I creative?

Considering yourself to be absolutely not creative is an indication of non-alignment of the Svadhisthana. Everyone's creativity is unique, but it should manifest itself in some way or the other.

Too Much

When excess energy flows into the sacral chakra, you'll be affected in the following ways:

- You'll overthink your past faults and emphasize them.

- You'll seek pleasure even when you have received sufficient enjoyment.

- You'll indulge in pleasurable activities more than focusing on other aspects of your life.

Not Enough

A lack of energy in the sacral chakra will affect you in the following ways:

- You wouldn't want to take part in creative activities.

- You'll lack sex drive.

- You might feel unloved or ignored by loved ones.

- Quite frequently, you'll be confronted by too many emotions.

Increasing Energy Flow

If your symptoms indicate that you lack energy flow in this chakra, you can attract more energy. Below are a few helpful suggestions.

Go to places where you can see nature in its glory. While this is always good advice, for the sacral chakra you should visit places near a water body. Spending time near a lake or by the river adjusts energy flow.

Make a routine for yourself and include time for creativity. Be careful not to be too serious about your creative activities. Take it lightly but enjoy it!

Maintain a journal. This is helpful when you can't figure out why your emotions are out to get you.

Lowering Energy Flow

To decrease the flow of energy in this chakra, concentrate on emotions and relationships.

Assess your relationship with others and understand the impact they have on you.

Try to read your emotions in connection with those of others and figure out how you are reacting to feelings.

Helpful Foods

Checking the gastronomic benefits of sacral chakra is not any less important. These are the foods you need to eat more to align the Svadhisthana chakra.

- carrots

- Mango

- Peaches

- Apricots

- Orange pepper

- Sweet potatoes

Notice that these fruits and veggies are orange as the color associated with the sacral chakra is orange. Keep in mind that if there's an excess of energy, you wouldn't need to completely cut down on these foods. They help in balancing the chakra; hence, they also have the potential to decrease the flow of energy.

Gems and Crystals

Some gems and crystals that have the power to remove blockages of the sacral chakra include:

- Crinoline: Orange in color, it stands for the vibrancy of spirit and creativity,

- Tiger's eye: It's earthly black and brown in color and represents creativity. It also helps you remain within bounds without sacrificing your fiery spirit.

- Amber: The color of this stone is orangish, and it contains healing energies required for clearing pathways for positivity.

Balancing the Chakra for Women

I've mentioned how the energy of this chakra holds special significance for women because imbalances often result in severe illnesses. To make sure your sacral chakra is aligned, you can do the following:

- Recognize your desires. Due to prejudices and preconceived ideas, women often shy away from expressing or even accepting their desires. Letting go of these notions isn't an easy process but the first step is to begin.

- Eating healthy and intermittent fasting is good for your overall health but especially for removing blockages from this chakra.

- Don't hesitate to explore new ways to be creative. Fear of failure might get in the way but tell yourself it doesn't matter if you fail. Learning and growing as a person are just as important!

Key Takeaways

You might be wondering if you're now equipped with all the information required to bring back balance in the Svadhisthana chakra. So, let's take a look back at what we've learned about the sacral chakra.

- This chakra is located in the lower abdominal region.

- It fosters creativity and helps in the fulfillment of desires.

- Emotional wellness and understanding your desires are key to balancing energies in this chakra.

- The color orange symbolizes the chakra so keeping orange crystals and eating foods that are of a similar color can be immensely beneficial.

Chapter 5:

Solar Plexus Chakra—Manipura

Progressing further, we'll find the solar plexus chakra or the Manipura. This chakra stimulates the fire within, so you are motivated to reach your goals. Are you eager to hit new targets and cherish new achievements? If the question made you sigh or roll your eyes sarcastically, your solar plexus chakra is not in balance.

Igniting your passions and ensuring you have the zeal for a better future, the Manipura chakra removes blockages that make you struggle with motivation. To be successful and happy, you need this chakra to be aligned. If you're successful but not happy, it's an indication that the Manipura chakra is not open, and you still feel less confident.

This chakra also controls digestion, so any problems in the alimentary system might be a result of an imbalance of energies in the Manipura. Food and exercise play a big role in monitoring energy flow to the solar plexus chakra. You'll learn more about this in the latter part of this chapter.

Introduction to the Solar Plexus Chakra

It's time to explore the basics of the Manipura chakra.

Location

The solar plexus chakra is located in the area of your stomach, slightly above the abdomen.

Color

Yellow denotes this chakra and to effectively perform balancing rituals, the color yellow must be present in some form.

Meaning

The third chakra increases your confidence and self-esteem. When you don't believe in your abilities or feel good about your performance at work or any other aspect of life, you can't truly flourish no matter how much you've outwardly achieved. So, in essence, this chakra helps you restore faith in yourself and cultivate a healthy attitude toward life.

Mantra

"Ram" is the mantra chanted in rituals or meditations on the solar plexus chakra. The word carries the message, "Self-love starts when I accept all parts of myself" (Yogi Cameron, 2021).

Element

The Manipura chakra is best expressed through fire. Solar plexus refers to the sun center, hence alluding to a fiery attribute. Now think about your motivation playlist. It must have a song about the fire within you. As you work out, complete your chores, or finish off tasks on your to-do list, you tap your feet to the beats of a song that instructs you to let the flame inside you grow into a fire. Passion is always connected to your inner fire, which is why it's the element representing the solar plexus chakra.

An Overview

Free energy flow to the third chakra ensures good health and high spirits. I think the best way to understand whether your solar plexus chakra is in alignment is to track your mood and judge how you're feeling about life at the moment. An optimistic outlook is likely indicative of a perfect balance of energies in this chakra.

The name Manipura translates as "jewel city", implying the self as a sparkling, bright space. You might not hold yourself in the highest esteem at the moment, but you are capable of much more than you think! The solar plexus chakra removes negative energies that bring your spirits down. It sends good vibrations through your system, enabling you to reach your full potential. Illnesses often stand in the way of your goals, so the Manipura chakra cures many illnesses and the troubles they bring with them.

A lotus with ten petals symbolizes the solar plexus chakra. Representing the ten pranas or vital forces that keep a tab on the vital forces of the body, this symbol reflects the power of the Manipura chakra. Another symbol, specifically relating to the energy emanated by this chakra, is a triangle with its top down. To put it simply, the symbol suggests the retainment of positive energies and outflow of negativity.

Imbalances in the Solar Plexus Chakra

Have you ever wondered why you keep getting sick with digestion problems even though you aren't eating anything that's bad for you? Well, one reason behind this can be blockages in the Manipura chakra. But digestion isn't the only issue that's indicative of imbalances in this chakra. Self-doubt, inability to trust others, tendency to seek validation and appreciation from others—these are pointers too.

Physical Signs of Blockage

Below are the illnesses and physical symptoms that would suggest the Manipura chakra is out of alignment.

- Improper processing of nutrients: you aren't able to enjoy the health benefits of the nutrients you're consuming because they aren't being processed in your system.

- Ulcers: A common symptom of non-aligned Manipura chakra, ulcers disrupt the entire digestive system and pose a great risk to general health.

- Irritable bowel syndrome: This is a fallout of indigestion. When the process is inconsistent and slow, your body tends to misread signals and you won't feel comfortable.

- Eating disorders: As your digestion is impacted by imbalances in the solar plexus chakra, you might develop eating disorders. The symptoms will vary, but in general, your relationship with food won't be healthy if you suffer from an eating disorder.

- Diabetes: Unhealthy or irregular eating is one of the main reasons why people develop type 2 diabetes. Now, when your Manipura chakra is not in alignment, you will be experiencing a wide range of digestive problems. As a result, you'll find yourself modifying your diet time and again. Ultimately, this might end up resulting in diabetes.

- Diseases of liver, pancreas, and colon: Your upper abdomen area is affected by solar plexus chakra imbalances. The organs located in this area suffer as a consequence. Be careful though, a liver or pancreas disease doesn't immediately suggest a disbalance of energies in the Manipura chakra. It's important to look at all the possible signs before coming to any conclusion because almost every chakra influences health.

Mental Health Signs

As you read in the previous chapters, mental health too is at a disadvantage when your chakras aren't aligned. For the solar plexus chakra, the signs of imbalance usually relate to a drop I'm creativity and hesitation to express yourself. Let's go over the symptoms in a little more detail.

- Hindrance to self-expression: Blocked energies stifle your ability to creatively express yourself. For example, let's say someone asked you to introduce yourself. You'll feel at a loss for words. Earlier, you might have been quite fluent when talking about your life. Why did this change suddenly? Something must be blocking positive energies from finding their way into the Manipura chakra.

- Aggressive behavior: Take a moment to reflect on how you've been interacting with friends, family, and strangers. Is there an underlying anger and frustration that you feel whenever asked to interact? Do you think you're getting more aggressive recently or have you been this way for quite some time now? Don't worry, this isn't a judgment of your character. The aggression stems from your inability to articulate your concerns and emotions. It's a sign that your solar plexus chakra is blocked.

- Listlessness: Motivation is often derived from bouts of creativity. You might be working a regular nine to five that doesn't require you to be creative, but everyone likes to add a dash of creativity to most things they do. Even if your work isn't particularly creative in nature, you could have been expressing it in other aspects of your life. However, when the solar plexus chakra is out of alignment, you'll settle in for a dull existence, not wishing to get involved in anything that needs creativity. Suppose your home needs redecorating, you won't feel the urge to look for unique decor ideas, you'll sigh and do the bare minimum.

- Controlling attitude: This is somewhat related to aggressiveness, but someone with a blocked Manipura chakra might try to be controlling in a suave manner too. What this type of behavior implies is simply your urge to be in control of situations and other people's reactions. Often, such an attitude develops from neediness, which we'll discuss next.

- Neediness: No, I'm not referring to your food cravings although that too might be a symptom of blockages in the third chakra. Here I'm referring to your need for validation. You won't be satisfied with what you do unless your efforts are validated by someone else. Lack of confidence contributes to this.

- Victim mentality: Let's suppose you aren't validated by others around you, this won't lead to immediate acceptance of shortcomings. Rather, you'll think you're the victim. Some people tend to believe that a victim mentality is ingrained and can't be changed, but let me tell you, that isn't accurate. Once the blockages are removed, you'll notice your mindset changing.

- Fear and lack of courage: You'll be gripped by this constant fear that won't let you try new things and find ways of being happy. At the back of your mind, a voice will be telling you, "What if I fail?". You might think you have the power to disregard this voice, but it isn't so simple. Consider what you've done recently, and you'll notice it's usually a known pattern of activities. Opening up the Manipura chakra will enable you to explore new avenues and reach your full potential.

Why You Should Remove Blockages From the Manipura

Until you align this chakra, you're robbing yourself of the chance to flourish. Be it your job, finances, or personal life, you won't be giving yourself the chance to get the best out of the opportunities that appear. Opening this chakra will help you find your capabilities. You won't be in the dark anymore, trying to figure out what you should do to change things around you. Once you know what you value most, you'll be able to set aside things that don't mean much to you. The classic example in this context is someone quitting their high-paid job, hoping to start a new, more meaningful life.

Removing Blockages

There are a number of ways in which you can modify the energy flow in the solar plexus chakra. Usually, lifestyle changes help a great deal. You'll, however, need to practice asanas and meditations for the best results.

Strength Your Digestive Fire

Effectively reducing digestive problems through simple solutions—that's the best way to remove blockages from the Manipura chakra. Below are a few tips.

- Drink water regularly and at room temperature. Too much or too little water can mess up the digestive process.

- Control portion sizes. Using cups to measure your meals will do away with the hassle of figuring out how much you should eat.

- Don't eat excessively spicy food. Avoid spicy food altogether if it doesn't suit you.

- Try to avoid drinking too much water while eating. Small sips should be fine. Resist the temptation to drink sparkling water, soda, or alcohol.

- Allow your body to rest between meals. Snacking a lot will prevent your body from digesting foods properly. It might also get in the way of weight loss. In this context, intermittent fasting is an excellent method to improve digestion and lose weight at the same time. Women, especially those above 50, benefit from fasting techniques. In my book Intermittent Fasting for Women Over 50, I have included several tips and tricks to reach your fasting goals and see results. Check it out if this is something that interests you.

Breathwork

Breathwork is good for both digestion and overall metabolism. Try the following breathing exercise to feel the digestive fire glow inside you.

Sit upright and relax your shoulders. Take a few deep breaths and relax. Next, inhale and exhale forcefully through your nose while keeping your lips closed. Once you've adjusted to this breathing pattern, take short breaths and exhale the same way through your nose. Repeating this 10 to 15 times will leave you feeling like you've just done an ab workout.

Asanas

The three asanas that are beneficial for your Manipura chakra are Navasana (boat pose), Matsayandrasana (seated spinal twist), and Warrior Pose.

- Navasana: The word "nava" in Sanskrit translates to boat. This pose is called so because your position will imitate the shape of a boat. For better understanding, though, you can think of the V shape. Sit on your mat, lean back slightly, and lift your legs up while keeping them straight. If you have a mirror, check if your pose is like a V. Helping with digestion and abdominal problems, the boat pose has been practiced by yogis for a very long time.

- Matsayandrasana: Translating to "the pose taken by the lord of the fishes." This asana is good for stretching and relaxation. It improves not only your physical health but also does wonders for mental health issues. Sit with both your legs forward. Then place the right foot on the left thigh so your heel presses against the naval. After twisting your torso to the left, hold your right ankle with your left hand.

- Warrior Pose: Chances are that you have already done this pose at some point because it's a common stretching exercise. Lunge forward and stretch your back leg, making sure it's straight. Once your legs are in the right position, extend one arm forward and the other backward. Remain in this position for a minute and then switch your legs—do a forward lunge with the other leg.

In Balance, Too Much, or Not Enough

We have reached that section where you get to ask yourself questions in order to decide if the energies in your solar plexus chakra are balanced.

In Balance

If you are in doubt, reflect on the following questions:

How do I perceive myself?

The answer will indicate if your self-esteem is high or lingering at the bottom. A distinction has to be made here between good self-esteem and overvaluing yourself. If it's the latter, it's possible that the energy levels are beyond what's necessary.

Am I able to make decisions without hesitating a lot?

Strong decision-making is a sign of balanced energies in this chakra. So, if you think your decision-making abilities are good, you might have a balanced Manipura.

Do I think I have an attractive personality?

A charismatic personality often suggests that all is well with your solar plexus chakra. Think about the aura you exude when you're out in public. Are you able to carry on interesting conversations with people for a considerable amount of time? You could be popular in your friend circles and also the person everyone flocks to. An affirmative response to this can also mean that your chakra is aligned.

Too Much

A few characteristics of people with too much energy in their solar plexus chakra are—swelling tempers, lack of control, and foul mood.

Tempers

Did anyone tell you that you have a quick fuse? Hold on a minute. You're not a disagreeable person who's always on their high horse. Temper issues are a common fallout of imbalances in the Manipura chakra. Next time you get angry, investigate the cause. If the underlying cause is minor or negligible, you should seriously consider improving balance in the third chakra.

Lack of Control

You might have felt helpless many times, frustrated at the absence of control over the things around you. Losing the power to control your situation is one of the worst feelings ever. If you regularly experience this, your solar plexus needs aligning.

Foul Mood

It isn't normal to be in a grumpy mood throughout the day. I understand that life gets in the way of good stuff, and you could be genuinely upset about something but that shouldn't last too long. If people are complaining that you're perpetually grumpy, alarm bells will start to ring asking you to check the flow of energy to the third chakra.

Not Enough

Although digestive issues are predominantly the common outcome of lack of energy in the solar plexus, other symptoms show up too. Here's a look at some of them.

Poor Appetite

Do you stare at your plate in disgust even if the food served is your favorite? Loss of appetite is typically a sign of energy imbalances in the solar plexus chakra. Compare your present food habits to how you ate in the past and note the differences. By relating the change to other events or symptoms, you'll be able to conclude whether energies are balanced.

Disorganization

When this chakra doesn't have sufficient energy, you will not be able to complete tasks on time and not be very organized with your duties.

Beneficial Foods for the Solar Plexus Chakra

Foods that are yellow in color like corn and fiber are especially helpful for the Manipura.

Crystals and Gems

You can use gems like Amber, Tiger's Eye, and Citrine that are also used for rituals involving the sacral chakra.

Key Takeaways

Here are the highlights of this chapter:

- The Solar Plexus Chakra controls your digestion. When it's not in alignment, you might have an unhealthy relationship with food.

- From a mental health perspective, the Manipura helps you become more courageous and confident, overcoming fear.

- Build a digestive fire within you through healthy eating and exercise to bring the energies in harmony.

The chakras we will discuss after this also have a deep spiritual significance. To heal completely, your ultimate goal should be self-realization and for this, you'll need to harness your spiritual powers. Let's start at the point where you realize your wishes and desires—the Heart Chakra.

Chapter 6:

Heart Chakra—Anahata

Being right in the middle, the heart chakra connects the lower chakras with those above. It's from here that you gradually step into the realm of spirituality, although it has a significant impact on your physical being as well. The name itself gives us an insight into what this chakra's role might be in our overall wellness. Yes, you must've guessed it already—energies in this chakra ensure heart health, at the same time acting as a center of empathy and kindness. When everything is alright with the Anahata, your cardiovascular health should be in top shape and your relationships will flourish. But misplaced energies and blockages could result in heart disease, asthma, or weight gain. From the perspective of relationships and love, blockages in the heart chakra cause people to compromise self-care to pay more attention to others and this could prove to be damaging to their mental health.

Introduction to the Heart Chakra

It's time to review the basic features of the heart chakra.

Location

The Anahata is located at the center of the chest, just above the heart. Sometimes, yogis refer to this area as the "heart center" (Stelter, 2016).

Color

Green is considered to be the color for the heart chakra. People who aren't familiar with the chakra system and color associations might think that surely the heart chakra will be represented by red. We see heart symbols in red and it's natural to come to this conclusion, but from the chakra point of view, green goes perfectly well with the Anahata. Green is representative of life and nature, the latter symbolizing rejuvenation and a calm temperament. If you remember from chapter 1, each chakra has a color that vibrates with the same frequency as the energies in it. The heart chakra has the same vibrations as the color green.

Balanced energies in the Anahata help in building a better relationship with nature. Being in close proximity to nature is also one of the best ways to balance these energies. As you'll see later in this chapter, peaceful meditation sessions in nature go a long way in removing blockages in the Anahata chakra.

Meaning

The heart is inextricably attached to feelings, and above all, it's responsible for love and compassion. Any problems in the heart chakra would be indicated by dissatisfaction with relationships or lack of self-love. A person with blockages in the Anahata wouldn't necessarily be unloving or unkind, more commonly, they end up loving or caring for others without reciprocation.

Mantra

"Yam" is the mantra chanted while meditating on the heart chakra. It translates to, "when I love myself, loving others comes easily" (Yogi Cameron, 2021). Without self-love, happiness isn't achievable. No matter how much you do for others, as long as you ignore your needs, you won't find true joy. Balancing the energies in the fourth chakra is essentially showing yourself some much-deserved love.

Element

The Anahata has air as its element because it stands for freedom and expansion (Yoga in Daily Life, 2021). As the chakra that is often thought to be the first step towards a spiritual journey, the heart chakra, and its element signifies ascension. The company of nature, also implying freedom, aids this journey.

A Brief Overview

Symbolized by a lotus with twelve petals, the Anahata is the seat of our "atma" or the divine self. Among the divine qualities of the heart, the most prominent are kindness, love, empathy, understanding, and harmony. We can't, however, dismiss the fact that our hearts can also harbor negative feelings and confused emotions. The heart chakra can be considered a confluence of divine qualities and personal emotions. Free-flowing and balanced energies keep everything in check, not allowing the personal completely overtake the divine qualities. Two star-shaped triangles appear in the image of the heart chakra. The points that are facing upward indicate spiritual ascension and the points facing down are negative emotions. As a consequence of imbalances, you could foster negative feelings such as jealousy, hatred, hopelessness, and desire to cause harm to others or yourself.

Speaking of desires, the Anahata gives you the capacity to fulfill your wishes and express creative talent. Focusing on your Sankalpa Shakti, or willpower that resides in your heart, you'll be able to witness the realization of your most cherished dreams. The antelope, an animal often thought to be representative of one's deepest desires, is the symbolic animal for the heart chakra. While it also stands for alertness and concentration, the antelope strongly suggests the progression toward your desired state in life.

Imbalances in the Heart Chakra

The fourth chakra has energies that regulate essential body functions related to the heart. Symptoms that indicate imbalances in the heart chakra relate to the upper body, not just the heart. The lungs, arms, chest, and hands might also experience problems when energies are blocked. Below is a discussion about the most prominent symptoms.

Physical Illnesses

The following signs and illnesses could suggest that your heart chakra is not in alignment:

Hypertension or high blood pressure is commonly associated with an imbalanced flow of energy in the heart chakra. We shouldn't, however, think that low blood pressure doesn't indicate the same. If your blood pressure is above or below the average rate, you have to consider whether it's stemming from imbalances of energies in your heart chakra.

Since the upper body is affected, any aches or pain you might feel in the region can be a symptom of blocked energies. It's wise to check for other symptoms as well because aches tend to result from various anomalies in the system.

Lung infections, bronchitis, and circulatory diseases are also signs of heart chakra blockages. If you constantly suffer from any of these, there's a chance the energies in the Anahata aren't perfectly aligned.

Mental Health Problems

Your emotions often lead to the crux of the matter. Maybe you are not able to maintain happy relations, or you prefer being isolated although it doesn't make you happy. This isn't a verdict on what type of a person you are, it can mean you have an imbalanced heart chakra. Here are a few signs that you should be aware of:

Loneliness: You don't want to be with people, but you don't feel good when you are alone. This might mean you are drifting away from others and creating a space for yourself that you're not ultimately comfortable with. Imbalances in the anahata often lead to this type of feeling.

Compromises: Do you find yourself doing better than your best for others, compromising your needs, even if you don't get enough in return? Sometimes this behavior is a result of an overflow of energy in the heart chakra.

Affected Relationships: Your relationships could be affected because you either put in too much effort or you feel defensive and fail to open up. Blockages in the Anahata cause you to hold grudges for a long time and be jealous of others. Don't be disheartened if you feel this way, there are fixes and I'll explain this later in the chapter. Negative emotions could make you think you aren't a good person in general but that's not true. You can change if you go about it the right way.

Lack of Trust: Now this isn't only about relationships, blocked energies also stop you from trusting people. You could have a fear of being hurt and thus hesitate before placing your faith in someone. When you start to heal, you'll start to focus more on yourself, figuring out why you lack trust.

Fear of Intimacy: Energies in the heart chakra unlock many positive emotions, especially love and kindness. Are you stuck in a quandary about whether or not you should be intimate with someone? Maybe it's the blocked energies that are holding you back.

Removing Blockages

Now that you know about imbalances, let's think about how you can remove the blockages. Of course, Asanas and meditation will play a role as always, but developing a loving temperament is the first step toward success here.

Be compassionate

Compassion is about understanding another person's situation and providing them with some form of help. You don't have to do anything extreme to show compassion, sometimes a kind word can go a long way too. I think a good starting point is looking at the people in your life and checking if they are doing well. Maybe your friend is going through a rough patch, or a family member has just experienced a tragic event. You can begin by truly understanding the difficulty of their situation and see if there's anything you can do to help.

Give Love to Receive Love

Balance is key to everything in life and it's no different where love or relationships are concerned. You might be that person who is always helping everyone despite not getting the same help when needed. On the other hand, you could be waiting for love while not realizing the fact that you aren't giving enough love in the first place. Balancing energies should start with decluttering your heart and making space for love and kindness.

Smile at people you meet through the course of your day, I assure you that will help you feel better as well. Share a few words with someone who needs a friend to talk to. Forget about past disappointments and don't hold onto resentments. Otherwise, you'll be bitter and never experience satisfaction. Another great way to fight off negativity is to avoid criticizing others unnecessarily. If you reflect on it, you'll see there are times when you criticize without reason, or even if there's a reason, you can express your critique constructively.

Practice Gratitude

Gratitude is essential for your overall well-being. Think of the last time someone did you a favor. Had you responded with a thank you? You can try doing it the next time. Trust me, it can be a truly fulfilling experience. According to research, gratitude doesn't only contribute to your personal happiness, it establishes a connection between you and the wider scheme of things (Berkeley, 2019).

Here are some ways to practice gratitude:

- Thank people who help you in your everyday life. Be it your family, friends, retail worker, a server, or even a random stranger who does something for you.

- Maintain a gratitude journal where you document the events that make you grateful. You can also have a jar where you throw in a few notes about the times you feel grateful.

- When you're upset about how things are going, read your journal. It'll give you an insight into what's right in your life and cheer you up. We sometimes forget the positive side when life takes a turn for the worse and reminding us of that side is one of the best ways to bring back harmony and happiness.

Asanas

Asanas that involve the upper body, especially the chest, are important for the removal of blockages. Some of these Asanas include:

Camel Pose

Also known as Ushtrashana, this pose helps you open your heart but also has an energizing quality. Back pains and tightness in your upper body are cured by the persistent practice of the camel pose. Generally speaking, this pose is a backbend, but remember to gently transition into it. First of all, sit on your knees and extend your hand backward, touching your toes. Gradually, do the backbend while focusing on your breathwork. If no attention is paid to breathing, yoga loses much of its significance. Follow and control your breathing without trying to hold it back for too long.

Standing Bow Pose

The name says what this Asana is all about. Extend one of your legs backward and hold it while you stretch the opposite arm forward. For best results, remain in the posture for some time and concentrate on your breathing. Check yourself in the mirror if you have one in the room because the pose could go wrong because of small errors.

Cow Face Pose

Gomukhasana or the cow face pose is called so because when you get into the posture, the structure formed will resemble a cow's face. Sit tall and cross your legs. Then stretch one of your arms upwards and the other backward. Let the arm that is stretched upwards fall back gradually so that the elbow faces the ceiling. When you believe the arm is stretched properly, hold the fingers with your other arm. This pose provides you with a good stretch and is good for fixing issues with posture. Of course, it also checks energy flow to the heart and brings balance.

Loving Kindness Meditation

Eve Eckman, Ph.D., introduced this meditation and many people have since benefited from it. Sometimes all you need to do is think about the love you've received or how kind someone has been to you. Even if you start out with negative feelings like resentment or jealousy, you are sure to end this session with a smile on your face and love in your heart.

Sit or lie down in a comfortable position. Play some soft music in the background if that helps you relax. Be careful not to be distracted during the session because you need to take in the experience fully in order for the results to manifest. Close your eyes and picture a person who loves you dearly and has always treated you with compassion. Imagine them sitting in front of you, beaming pleasantly. Kindness radiates from them and fills your heart. Feel this loving kindness inside you when you reflect on their actions toward you. Once you believe you have understood the nature of their love, slowly let their image fade away from your mind. What are you left with? A bout of positivity and a lot of love!

Heart Chakra Affirmations

Affirmations help you develop confidence in yourself and redirect your attention to positive thoughts. You can practice affirmations for any chakra. However, since the Anahata is more concerned with emotions and mindset, including affirmations in your routine will open the chakra and receive sufficient energy flow. Base your affirmations around forgiveness, gratitude, love, and self-care. Below are some examples.

- I will not think about past mistakes because I've overcome them.

- I don't hold anything against people who have wronged me before.

- Today, I'll take care of myself and love myself for who I am.

- I'll open myself to love and reciprocate the generosity shown by others.

- I'll smile and try to make others happy however I can.

- I won't spend time worrying about people who've been cold towards me.

- My feelings are valid, and I'll try to understand them better.

In Balance, Too Much, or Not Enough

Like we've done for the previous chakras, we have to consider why your heart chakra might not be in alignment. Although by now, you might have some idea about what could be wrong, you still need to ask yourself some questions to verify. We will begin with the questions that will tell you whether everything is okay.

In Balance

How did you react when someone mentioned love or compassion? That's a good opening question for you to get started. Your reaction will speak volumes about the energies in your heart chakra. This, however, is a broad topic, so I've provided a breakdown.

Do I feel compassionate towards others?

If you're having trouble understanding other people's situations and you fail to show empathy, chances are very high that your heart chakra is out of alignment. An open heart allows you to empathize and be compassionate. Let's say you've recently learned that a friend is going through a difficult time but you don't approach them with a few kind words, you lack the energies that would shape the emotions required in this case.

Am I always giving love without caring about myself?

While giving love is good and necessary, you also need to see whether you are receiving enough. Energy imbalances are created when you compromise your needs continuously. You can simply observe your daily life to realize whether you are being appreciated for the effort you're putting in.

Do I feel accepted?

Isolation is a sign of imbalance if that isolation is causing you to be lonely and unhappy. Inspect the role of everybody in your life and your relationship with them. Do you tend to move away from people who care because you think they might not accept you? Do you avoid groups and communities because you fear not being able to fit in? That indicates problems with energy flow in the heart chakra.

Too Much

You know how to detect imbalances. It's time now to check if the scales are on the heavier side.

Jealousy

Sometimes it's possible to be jealous without even realizing it. The answer lies in how you react to the successes of others. Do you feel bad when your friend achieves something big just because you don't have the same accomplishment? In that case, you are jealous, and it could be triggered by unwanted energies in the heart chakra. You want to attract positivity your way and get upset when others enjoy the same.

Don't worry, as I always say, this doesn't mean you're a bad person. You are sheltering negativity in you and it's time to let that go.

Clinginess

Being too possessive can lead to problems in relationships and friendships that you cherish. Because you love and care for someone, you might get too attached to that person and not realize that it's having a bad fallout. Imbalanced energies cause this kind of clingy behavior to spiral out of control.

Not Enough

What if there's a lack of energy in the Anahata? Here are the symptoms.

Shyness or Loneliness

Shyness might be a personality trait but if you find that it's standing in the way of your happiness, it's serious. Your heart gives you the confidence to mingle with others and enjoy a thriving social life. So, when there's a lack of energy here, it will naturally influence how you interact.

If you're lonely most of the time, it could suggest you are not allowing for deeper connections and shying away from being with others. The best way to determine if this is a problem is to consider how often you are alone and what it makes you feel.

Inability to Forgive

Holding grudges interferes with wellness. So, if you are not able to forgive, you are denying yourself the chance to be truly happy. This can stem from a lack of energy flow in the Anahata. The expression "having a big heart" has something to do with this. When you are doing your best to remove the Blockages, you are harnessing the power to forgive which is a superpower in many ways.

How to Increase Energy Flow

Below are some suggestions that will help you if your heart chakra lacks energy flow.

- Affirmations that assert confidence and self-love are extremely helpful for increasing energy in the heart chakra.

- The color pink attracts energy to the Anahata. Wear something pink or use pink quartz during meditation sessions.

- Try using rose essential oils because they are magnetic as far as positive energies are concerned.

- Practice meditations similar to the loving-kindness meditation.

How To Decrease Energy Flow

Don't fret if you fear the energies in your heart chakra are a bit overwhelming. You can do the following:

- Write entries in your gratitude journal or simply think about the things you're grateful for.

- Drive your thoughts away from negativity and focus on love, empathy, and compassion.

- Talk to people about happy memories and share peaceful moments with family or friends.

Foods to Remove Blockages

Eating habits count when your aim is to align all your chakras. Since the heart chakra is associated with the color green, you should eat green veggies and fruits for the best results. Broccoli, kale, celery, parsley, matcha, Avocado, lime, mint, peas, kiwi, green apples, zucchini, and cucumber are good, and you can include as many of them in your meal as you like.

Gems and Crystals

Crystals are important for meditations and having green as its color, the heart chakra has vibrations that resonate with green gems. However, pink is also often associated with the Anahata. Some of the most effective crystals to use for your meditations would include:

Rose quartz: Colored light or vivid pink and also called the "heart stone." Rose quartz helps build relationships, relieves anxiety, makes you compassionate, and brings good fortune.

Emerald: This green stone represents domestic happiness and the joy of love. It's used in rituals to improve relationships.

Rhodonite: When your intention is to spread love in the world around you, Rhodonite is the stone you should pick. Pinkish in color, it removes blockages and fills your heart with love.

Amazonite: Assisting with trauma healing and removal of fear, this greenish-blue stone enables the heart to receive love.

Key Takeaways

Let's take another look at the highlights of this chapter.

- The heart chakra, being in the middle, is a point of connection between the first and the last three chakras. It's considered the first step to spiritual ascension.

- Energy imbalances cause illness relating to the upper body and emotional problems that can affect relationships.

- Along with asanas and meditation, practicing gratitude, showing compassion, and opening yourself to kindness from others are ways to bring the energies in tune.

- Green and pink crystals are used in rituals for harmonizing energies.

When your heart gives you a signal, you try to express that feeling. Keeping that in mind, let's look at the fifth chakra which has a lot to do with your communicative abilities.

Chapter 7:

Throat Chakra—Vishuddha

Verbal communication is the essence of the fifth chakra. Energies in the Vishuddha allow us to be expressive and establish clarity in our method of communication. Of course, it also influences the throat region physically too. In the previous chapter, compassion stands out as an important factor for wellness. But how would you show compassion if you aren't able to express yourself in the way you'd like to?

I'll give you a few examples to throw more light on the role of the throat chakra. Have you ever been in a situation where you wanted to say something but couldn't figure out how to phrase it? Well, this could be a result of blockages present in the throat chakra. On the other hand, you might be at another extreme where you're vocal even when you don't need to be. Maybe you chime in and dominate conversations, undermining others. Although it might not be your intention and you could be just showing enthusiasm, this could upset others and damage your relationships. With the right amount of energy in the fifth chakra, you won't have these problems.

The Basics

Here's a look into the important features of the throat chakra.

Location

Situated in the area of your throat, this chakra moderates voice and conversations.

Meaning

At the core of this chakra is its power to aid healthy communication. You might have several great ideas, but they won't be fruitful if you can't translate them into action. Similarly, without communication, thoughts don't have the same value.

Mantra

Roughly interpreted as, "I speak my truth, always", the mantra "HAM" encourages unhindered self-expression. As long as you stay true to your beliefs and articulate them fearlessly, you'll be content, no matter what others say. Finding your voice is hard but once you do so it's a liberating experience and the Vishuddha chakra is instrumental in making that happen.

Color

Blue or turquoise is the color of the Vishuddha chakra. In essence, the color is reminiscent of purity. Vishuddha means purity and the vibrations of the color blue or aquamarine go well with the deep significance of the chakra.

The Vishuddha is responsible for spiritual awakening and purity of the soul is necessary to attain this state. Self-awareness comes with the purification of your soul and dispelling of unwanted affections. The truth takes precedence over falsities and the throat chakra brings this truth to the forefront.

Element

The element of this chakra is sound or music. Although some Hindu philosophies consider Akasha or space to be the element of the throat chakra because it acts as a stepping stone to spirituality through purification.

A Brief Overview

To symbolically represent the Vishuddha chakra, a lotus with sixteen petals is usually drawn for rituals. There are various interpretations of the sixteen petals. They can be regarded as the sixteen abilities a person has the ability to develop. Since the throat chakra controls communication, the sixteenth petals are also considered to be the sixteen vowels of the Sanskrit alphabet. Vak Siddhi or the ability to make your words come true is possible through the regulation of energies in this chakra.

Vishuddha chakra is the center of the Udana Prana which purifies the body through breathwork. Spiritual cleansing is also achieved through balanced energy flow in this chakra. Represented by Brahma, the Creator of the universe, the Vishuddha chakra leads you to higher levels of spirituality. But this chakra will also help you in your everyday life. With a new sense of freedom and the courage to voice your truth, you'll succeed in honing your skills to perfection.

Imbalances in the Throat Chakra

Unless the energy flow to the throat chakra is balanced, you'll experience physical problems with your throat and a mental blockage when it comes to expressing yourself.

Physical Signs

Below are the illnesses that indicate a possible imbalance in this chakra.

- Thyroid: Both hypothyroidism and hyperthyroidism are caused by imbalances.

- Hoarseness of voice and other difficulties with speaking often result from issues in this chakra.

- Sore throat or sores in the mouth can be a sign of blockages. Observe if this is a recurring matter because that would suggest your throat chakra is not in alignment.

- Gum diseases, ear infections, and sinuses are health problems that most people deal with frequently. Although other contributing factors may be present, imbalanced energies in the Vishuddha chakra are a possible answer to why you can't find a lasting cure.

- You might experience tight shoulders and issues with your Temporomandibular joint (TMJ) tissues.

Mental Health Signs

Blockages in the chakra stop you from speaking your mind but they can also have the opposite effect and cause you to keep talking even when your input is not required in a certain situation. Below are the most prominent mental health-related signs of blockages in the fifth chakra.

Shyness and Anxiety About Speaking

Think about how you react when you desperately want to say something but feel the jitters. Either that or you're unable to find the right words to say. Fear of public speaking and general anxiety to articulate your thoughts stems from blockages in the Vishuddha chakra. You could be holding back opinions and ideas because you think they aren't good enough or don't know how best to phrase them. Remember that you might actually know ways to voice them but believe that's not good enough.

Do you also think twice before asking a friend for something or simply talking to people you care about? The inhibition you feel perhaps isn't relegated to public speaking but personal conversations as well. It could create a lot of damage because people won't always understand what's going on with you.

Speaking Too Much

Contrarily, you might have a tendency to speak out of line or use inappropriate language. This too is a sign of a blockage in the throat chakra. You might start out with a clear idea but as you speak you could lose track. Though it happens to everyone at some point, when it becomes more regular, you know there's something wrong.

Dominating Conversations

People with blockages in the throat chakra often get into arguments because they don't allow the other person to speak. Just as the inability to say what you want is a problem, this habit of dominating conversations is harmful and might turn others away from you.

Why It's Important to Bring Balance in the Throat Chakra

Without balance in this chakra, you won't achieve overall healing. Suppose your heart chakra is aligned and you want to be kind to others. But how will you do it if you fail to express that? You could have gained confidence by balancing energies in the root chakra. But where would this confidence lead? You won't be able to truly understand what you want and be at peace. To progress to the chakras located above the Vishuddha, you'd need the throat chakra to be working well. Spiritual upliftment won't be possible without the throat chakra.

Removing Blockages

Aside from breathwork and meditation, you have to adopt a new perspective to open the throat chakra. Despite requiring long-term dedication, it's not complicated. Here's what you can do:

Determine Your Highest Truth

First things first, you should understand what "highest truth" refers to in this context. It's the ultimate truth about who you are and what you want from life. When you're getting started, it doesn't need to assume a spiritual or esoteric significance. Your truth is what you believe to be right, it constitutes your personality. People often get confused between their truth and what others or society as a whole upholds as ultimate virtues. Based on what others want to hear, you might be tempted to alter your true beliefs and perception.

I know this task seems daunting in the initial stages but if you have already balanced your energies in the other chakras, the truth will gradually become clear to you. Your root chakra consolidates your foundation, and the sacral chakra bolsters your confidence while the heart chakra enables you to make sense of your emotions. These are steps that bring you closer to your true goals. When the blockages in your throat chakra are removed, you'll succeed in determining goals for wellness.

Express Your Truth

Are you one of those people who always go with the flow of conversations without highlighting their perspective? To accommodate the needs of others, you might be forgetting the importance of self-expression. Don't worry, it happens to everyone. But after a point, it can slowly hinder your agency and you'll find yourself reiterating the points of view shared by others instead of your authentic perception of things. Needless to say, after a certain point, you'd think you have failed to carve a niche for yourself despite getting chances to do so. Each person is unique and their way of looking at life has a new angle. Unless you emphasize your unique viewpoint, you won't feel accomplished.

Blockages in the throat chakra prevent you from expressing your truth, however, one of the ways to remove these blockages is to start asserting this truth. Before you are able to say it out loud, you must tell yourself that this is what you believe in. Convince yourself by arguing for your opinions and establishing the need to make others aware. Once you have mustered the courage, you can start speaking to others about your beliefs. Remember to not override others but to subtly introduce your opinions. For example, if you are with a group of friends and everyone has agreed with something that you don't think is right, you can politely tell them how you feel. Absolutely disregarding them would paint you in a dim light which you don't want.

Speak and Listen With Compassion

Following up on the last point, it's necessary to understand that your words are powerful. They can inspire, soothe, and provide comfort, but they might cause hurt as well. Does this mean you will let those words remain unspoken, thinking about consequences? No, that would defeat the purpose. You should always consider the context first—decide whether you are required to speak or if your contribution is needed, and how best to frame your speech so it doesn't affect anyone negatively. A large part of how you speak also depends on your ability to listen. If you're a good listener, you'll judge the scenario accurately, gauge the feelings of others involved, and only then speak your mind.

To simplify matters, let me list some questions you should ask yourself before you speak:

Do I know exactly what I'm going to say?

Not knowing this can escalate the situation if you choose to take your speech in an unplanned direction.

Is my input required here?

Sometimes you are part of conversations where personal matters are discussed about which you might not have enough knowledge. Under such circumstances, it's best to listen and observe before sharing your thoughts/

How can I be kind when I speak?

Once you have decided that you do have an opportunity to speak, roughly phrase your sentences in your head, just to check if they are kind and compassionate towards the listeners. Think about how you'd feel if someone spoke to you in the same manner. I'm not suggesting you should always second guess yourself and moderate your truth to please others. But be sure not to hurt anyone in the process.

Asanas

For the physical benefits of the throat chakra alignment, you can practice the following asanas.

Bridge Pose

Also known as the Setu Bandha Asana or the pose that bridges the gap, this yoga routine helps you stretch and open pathways for energies to enter or leave the throat chakra. This is a supine pose and a type of backbend. You can use a mat for this exercise and also place a blanket under your shoulders for protection if you have any problems in that area. You should be lying on your back with your knees bent and your legs and feet parallel. Bring your feet closer to your buttocks and raise your hips. Be in this position for at least 30 seconds and control your breathing. The bridge pose helps with lower back pains, strengthens the core, and also opens your heart chakra. When you inhale and exhale slowly in this posture, you open blockages in the throat.

Shoulder Stand

Sarvangasana or the shoulder stand is a yoga pose that takes the whole body into account. In fact, the Sanskrit word translates to "an asana that incorporates the entire body". For beginners, this pose might be a little hard at first, but with regular practice, you'll be able to do it better. Lie down on a mat and gradually lift your lower body. Try to keep your legs straight and you'll notice how the shoulder region seems to bear the weight of your lower body. Apart from being a good stretch, the shoulder stand can improve your breathwork. When you practice controlled breathing in this posture, you put more effort into it than you do for other yoga poses. Both the upper and lower body muscles are strengthened through this pose.

Plow

An important pose in Hatha Yoga practice, the plow or Halasana is good for the throat chakra because it strengthens the diaphragm. Now, remember that all the poses you practice not only help you with physical pain and illnesses but also clear mental blocks. Focusing on your energies will become an easier process after you do this pose regularly. Looking at pictures of this pose, you might think it's too complicated, but trust me, once you learn how to do it, you'll want to practice it every day for the amazing benefits it provides. You can actually begin this with the shoulder stand and then slowly lower your legs back behind your head until your toes touch the ground. Support your shoulder with blankets because they will be holding your weight. Remain in the position for as long as you're comfortable and observe your breath.

Pranayama

Breathwork or pranayama is crucial for removing blockages in the fifth chakra. Since this is about your throat and the diaphragm, you should focus on breathing methods that provide optimal benefits for this region. Two breathing techniques are discussed below.

Ujjayi Breath

The word Ujjayi means victorious in Sanskrit. Hence, this breathing method means victorious breath. Having a number of benefits, the ujjayi breath technique is practiced in the Hatha Yoga tradition. With your lips sealed, breathe in and out through your nose. As you proceed, inhale more deeply and exhale slowly by constricting the muscles at the back of your throat (Eisler, 2016). To make sure you exhale in the right manner, practice once with your mouth open. When your mouth is open, exhale, making the sound "HAAAH". Afterward, do the same without opening your mouth. So, you'd be thinking about making the sound.

Among the major benefits of this breathing technique are tension relief, free flow of Prana, detoxification of the mind, and an increase in self-awareness (Eisler, 2016). It also provides relief from chronic throat problems once you start doing it accurately.

Lion's Breath

If you are looking for a pranayama that helps with thyroid, lion's breath is the best option. It also strengthens the vocal cord, clears your throat, and relaxes your face muscles. To determine your truth as you read earlier in the chapter, you need to free yourself of inhibitions and increase self-consciousness. Lion's breath can help you with both.

Sit in a comfortable position and start breathing in and out slowly. You should be leaning forward slightly and resting your hands on your knees or on the floor with your fingers open. Focus your gaze on something in front of you that is not too distracting. Inhale through your nose and when you exhale, stick your tongue out so it touches your chin. You should make a HA sound when exhaling. Repeat this five to seven times and end with regular controlled breathing for about three minutes (Cronkleton, 2020).

In Balance, Too Much, or Not Enough?

If you have already realized that your throat chakra needs balancing, it's time to check whether there is an excess or shortage of energy flow.

In Balance

Doubts always remain unless you're able to clear them with finality. In order to do that, you have to ask yourself some inevitable questions. You've done this exercise for the previous chakras, so now your task is to answer the questions below after giving them some thought.

Do you think you are authentic when you speak?

If your chakra is in balance, you won't feel that you're taking recourse to falsities when speaking. What you say might not be an outright lie, but you could be saying it to impress others or please them. Maybe on the odd occasion, your truth itself could be pleasing to others. But mostly, people alter their true opinion for the sake of others which is detrimental to their well-being.

Are you confident when speaking?

You should consider your confidence levels when you speak because inhibitions are a sure sign of energy disbalance in your throat chakra. Next time you talk to someone, notice how you're replying. Do you hesitate before you share your thoughts? Maybe you talk yourself out of heart-to-heart because that would require you to speak at length. Even if you aren't a shy person in general, conversations might seem tricky to you when the fifth chakra is out of alignment.

Are you a good listener?

At the other end of this is the tendency to jump to dialogue without paying attention to what someone else has to say. Notice whether you frequently make your way into conversations before another person has finished talking. What you say without listening might be inappropriate or hurtful, and maybe this is why people seem distant from you. A balanced throat chakra helps you improve your listening skills and get better at resolving conflicts in conversations.

Too Much

Concentration of excessive energies in the throat chakra leads to negative behavior. Here are some signs to watch out for:

Arrogance

Arrogance pushes people apart and holds you back from thriving in social scenarios. An energy overload in the Vishuddha chakra will cause you to behave arrogantly—you might dismiss opinions, think too highly of yourself, or be rude to others for no reason.

Manipulative behavior

If your actions are based on manipulation because you want to safeguard your interest, you might be suffering from blockages in the throat chakra. Suppose a person actively tries to win the trust of somebody by lying to them now and again, the former is being manipulative. I think it's best to analyze what goes through your mind before you speak or interact. Reflect on the last time you took recourse to lies and why you did it. Now think about whether you do it frequently. Your reflections will help you realize if you could potentially have excess energy in the Vishuddha chakra.

Talkativeness

Having too much energy in this chakra makes you talkative. Not that it causes any major harm like arrogance or manipulation, but it can disrupt conversations or annoy some people. The most significant consequence is what it does to you. Since a talkative person isn't usually able to remain quiet for long, they find it difficult to concentrate during meditation sessions. You know that meditation is an integral part of chakra healing. So, a talkative nature can be a threat to the healing process.

Not Enough

Now let's look at the flip side. What happens when there's a lack of energy in the throat chakra? Below are some conspicuous signs.

Hesitation

Do you think a lot but communicate very little? Blockages in the Vishuddha chakra stop you from expressing yourself clearly although you might know perfectly well what you need to say. Even when you say what's on your mind, chances are you won't explain everything that you want to.

Dearth of Cohesive Ideas

We don't always have great ideas but if someone notices that they can't bring thoughts together, it suggests an anomaly in the fifth chakra. Communication is only possible when you know what to say and as we've seen, knowing your truth is the first step.

Isolation

People who aren't successful communicators often opt to isolate themselves. You'll be upset but still choose to avoid the company of people because you aren't confident about how to interact.

Beneficial Foods

Berries, coconut, herbal teas, raw honey, apples, pears, and lemon are food stuff that aids the throat chakra. Citrus fruits are especially helpful because they cure colds and throat infections.

Crystals and Gems

I've listed the common crystals and gems used in rituals for the throat chakra. Since the color of this chakra is blue, usually the gems that have the right vibrations are blue or purple in color.

Amazonite: Bluish green and thought to be a medium for purification, this crystal brings emotional balance by calming the nervous system and ridding you of unwanted thoughts.

Turquoise: Another bluish-green gem, Turquoise helps you express yourself clearly.

Aquamarine: This crystal has the same color as the blue-green sea. It encourages honesty and improves connections.

Lapis Lazuli: Your ways of communicating become more lucid and expressive when you use this blue gem in your rituals.

Key Takeaways

In this chapter, you've learned about the gift of communication and how the throat acts as an energy center for it. Let's take a look at the highlights.

- Imbalances in this chakra might cause thyroid problems, throat infections, and speech defects.

- Blockages stop you from communicating properly, either inhibiting conversations or encouraging arrogant behavior.

- Trying to understand your true goals and practicing good communication strategies should work towards removing the blockages.

- Pranayama is important to align this chakra. Practice ujjayi breath and lion breath for positive results.

I'm sure you are all ready to take this on and heal your throat. So, now we'll be heading towards the upper chakras that assist your spiritual development.

Chapter 8:

Third Eye Chakra—Ajna

Also referred to as the brow chakra because of its location, the third eye chakra is responsible for intuition. I have seen people react in surprise when they hear about this chakra because the third eye is a concept that not everyone is well acquainted with. While the other chakras are named after their location, the primary name of this chakra has been derived from its spiritual significance. Confusion surrounding the meaning of the third eye can hurt a person's chances of balancing energies in this chakra. So, let's first understand what the third eye refers to.

Since it's not a physical reality, the third eye refers to intuition and your ability to perceive the truth about your surroundings. Simply speaking, you are able to see the big picture with the help of your third eye. Let's say you are going through a difficult period in your life and the tragic circumstances are not letting you look beyond them. Your third eye will allow you to glimpse the possibilities of happiness and peace that exist beyond these sad times. People whose Ajna chakra is blocked will be physically affected by headaches and inattentiveness. They could also have tunnel vision which doesn't facilitate a healthy lifestyle.

Introduction to the Third Eye Chakra

Here's all the basic information you need to know about the Ajna.

Location

The third eye chakra is located on your forehead, between your brows. Hindu mythological figures like Goddess Durga are typically seen with the third eye.

Meaning

Intuition is at the core of this chakra, but it also stands for wisdom and imagination. Looking at the big picture is a sign of wisdom because you aren't letting small failures define you. Think about it—the very image of the third eye is an imaginary concept, and it is so because this chakra fosters imagination.

Some people believe that when your third eye opens, you'll immediately have a spiritual experience. While this chakra does encourage spiritual growth, the results won't be the same for everyone. Maybe you won't be able to exactly predict the future, but the goal is to look forward to it. Be inspired to seek more knowledge and explore because your third eye will enable exploration!

Mantra

AUM, the mantra for the third eye, translates to, "I am open to exploring what cannot be seen" (Yogi Cameron, 2021). This chant is an expression of your desire to not limit yourself to visible reality. The third eye kindles your adventurous spirit and gives you a nudge to discover unique perspectives.

Color

Indigo is the color of the Ajna. It's a combination of royal blue and purple. This color has a twofold meaning. In one sense, it represents peace and calm. You need to be at peace with yourself and in harmony with nature if you want to see what isn't visible to the naked eye. The second significance of the color has links to its use in spiritual practices. It stands for the transition from life to death and then to another realm. Because this chakra is one of our main connections to the spiritual world, indigo is the perfect color to use in rituals.

Element

Light affects our vision more than anything else. Similarly, our spiritual vision will be guided by spiritual light. I know you have guessed already—the element of the third eye chakra is light.

A Brief Overview of the Ajna

The three Nadis Ida (Moon), Pingala (Sun), and Sushuma (Central) combine in the third eye chakra to establish Samadhi or supreme concentration. The other name for it, Ajna or Agya, means command. When this chakra commands, you are able to get a glimpse of the spiritual world.

A lotus with two petals symbolizes the chakra because only two levels of consciousness are acknowledged here—Atma (Self) and Paramatma (God). Shiva and Shakti or Goddess Durga are the deities of this chakra. When focusing on the Ajna, we must realize that visible reality or nature and divinity or supreme consciousness are already united but there is still a gap that needs to be filled.

Each chakra has several qualities and the three qualities that stand out for the Ajna are truth, emptiness, and bliss. Once you gain knowledge about the eternal truth, feelings that trouble you in the real world will no longer exist, so you'll be empty or in other words, in complete harmony. Our egocentric intellect might be stopping us from recognizing the higher power of reasoning or discernment (Viveka). Hence, we should attain enough knowledge to see beyond egocentrism.

Imbalances in the Third Eye Chakra

Blockages in the third eye chakra will result in you losing the connection with your wisdom and inner knowledge. While physical Signs relate to the brain and eyes, mental health can be impacted in a number of ways, mainly leading you to be too invested in minor problems of life.

Physical Signs

Illnesses pertaining to the brain, eyes, and sinuses are the main indicators of blockages. Some of the illnesses include:

- Vision Problems: You won't be able to see clearly or could experience strain in your eyes.

- Headaches: Frequent headaches and migraines are common for people whose third eye chakra is blocked. Since the chakra is located in the forehead, that's the worst affected area.

- Dizziness: You might feel dizzy out of the blue or it could persist for longer. Sometimes nausea accompanies dizziness.

- Clogged Sinuses: Sinuses cause a lot of pain and weakness. If you have clogged Sinuses, you will also have difficulty thinking clearly and numbness.

- Hearing Issues: You could have trouble hearing if the Ajna is blocked. Pain in the ears and infections follow.

- Memory Loss: The third eye chakra not only helps you look at the bigger picture, but it also ensures sound memory. Blockages here may cause memory loss and depletion of cognitive abilities. Owing to memory loss, you could also be confused about your present reality. Ultimately, a person is likely to have dementia in the later stages of life if blockages aren't cleared.

- Anxiety: Although it's a common symptom of energy flow issues, anxiety heightens when the energies in the third eye are imbalanced.

- Nightmares and Insomnia: Sleep becomes scarce because of anxiety and continuous lack of sleep causes insomnia. But one of the most prominent signs of imbalances in the sixth chakra is frequently occurring nightmares. Now, these nightmares don't have a pattern for everyone and typically depend on existing problems or worries in your life.

Mental Health Signs

Anxiety is one of the predominant signs of misdirected energy flow to the Ajna chakra. However, other symptoms are also present that could affect your well-being.

Inability to Envisage a Better Future

You have seen how the third eye awakens you spiritually but looking beyond present problems also means envisaging a bright future, which you won't be able to do if the energies are blocked. For example, you are not well and are bothered by chronic illnesses. With an optimistic mind, you'll be able to believe in a better future where healing is possible. With a blocked Ajna chakra, you'll be constantly worried and never capable of dreaming of a healthier tomorrow. Let me assure you though, that tomorrow can definitely be a reality, mainly through the clearing of the sixth chakra.

Foggy Mind

Your mind will keep you in panic mode because most of the time it will fail to figure out what's going on. A clear solution won't present itself before you. Let's say you're trying to help somebody but even after a day's worth of brainstorming you still can't decide what would work. It's not because you don't have the intelligence; your mind is foggy, saturated with too many thoughts, and you aren't succeeding in picking out the solution due to these intermingling thoughts.

Why You Should Remove Blockages

Aligning the third eye chakra is a must for spiritual development, notwithstanding its contribution to overall healing. To achieve mental clarity and adopt an optimistic way of thinking, you should make sure the energies in this chakra are balanced.

Removing Blockages

The good news is you can call upon your inner powers to balance the sixth chakra. If you're thinking that's a long shot, hear me out. Any meditation takes you on a journey to the depths of your mind, offering you many revelations along the way. So, when you're stuck, you have to search those very depths to find a way out.

Cultivate Your Sixth Sense

We normally make use of our five senses and take it for granted that the sixth sense is only an attribute for a select few. That is incorrect.

We all have the sixth sense, only some of us can experience it more than others. In ancient times, humans used to depend partly on their sixth sense to guide them because there were no aids to the five senses like in the world of today. Our system is built in a way that we can access this hidden power if we dig deeper.

I'll give you one tip that will go a long way in helping you foster your intuitive abilities—trust your instincts or that feeling in your gut. For example, suppose you have met somebody for the first time and although everything seems great, you have a hunch something is off about that person. Of course, you shouldn't just refuse to interact with them! But try to understand why you felt that way and gather more knowledge. Your intuition won't lead you astray.

Tap Into Your Inner Knowledge

You have a great reserve of knowledge inside you. When you tap into it, a vast majority of truths can be revealed to you. Not everyone has the right skill set to derive all that knowledge. But with apt questions and an intense willpower to seek, you'll make discoveries that will surprise you.

When you have a problem, ask yourself if that problem has cropped up before. How did you resolve it before? Your mind will automatically direct you to the answer if you reflect on it for long enough. I get that the problem itself might not be clear to you or you could be confused about your emotions at the time. The best option is to do a chakra meditation. When you focus your attention on the other chakras with the belief that you'll surely find out where the issue lies, your Ajna chakra will make you aware of it.

Asanas

Three yoga poses help with removing blockages in the third eye. Hatha yoga practitioners employ various techniques to activate the energies in the third eye and increase the capacity to see beyond what's apparent.

However, we are going to look at three main poses that you can benefit from.

Child's Pose

Balasana or the child's pose is often used as a cool-down exercise. It helps you stretch and relax. Only when you are in a state of relaxation can you have clarity of vision. Sit in a kneeling position and part your knees slightly. Raise your arms above your head, then gradually bring them down in front of you. It's best if you crawl forward and relax your core as you do so. Remember to control your breathing.

Dolphin Pose

Also called Makarasana, this yoga pose is dynamic and great for relieving stress. It also strengthens your body and improves bone health. You might be wondering why it's good for the third eye. Well, it reduces anxiety and aids depression besides giving you comfort from nagging pains! Anxiety and depression stand in the way of your ascent into the spiritual world. So, you need to get them out of the way, and doing the Dolphin Pose is a good start. To be in this posture, begin by lying face down. Then balance your upper body on your arms and get on your knees. Slowly, so as to not hurt any joints or muscles, lift your hips. Your shoulders should be at an equal distance, your forearms should be on the ground, and your palms should be face down. Check yourself in the mirror to see if your pose reminds you of a dolphin!

Eagle Pose

The eagle pose or Garudasana helps you focus and increases your power of concentration. You'll need to start by standing with a slight bend in your knees. Lift one leg and bring it closer to your chest. Cross the lifted leg over to the other thigh. Your toes should be facing down. One of your arms should be wrapped around the other and your palms should be pressed together. That's it, you're in the perfect position!

Like most poses, the Garudasana stretches your muscles, but it also increases body awareness.

Mantras

Your third eye chakra can be brought into alignment through mantra chanting. Since it has a deep spiritual significance, mantras are especially helpful in balancing energies in the sixth chakra. You can call these mantras affirmations as well because their goal is to help you assert your belief in inner knowledge. I have listed some affirmations below:

I know my intuition is right and I give it the power to guide me.

The energies in my body and mind are in perfect balance.

True knowledge is within me and if I search thoroughly enough, I'll find it.

Sound Healing: The Humming Bee Sound

Through sounds and breathing techniques, you can focus energies on your third eye chakra. The Humming Bee Sound is good for increasing concentration and tapping into the pool of inner knowledge. Sit in a comfortable position, close your eyes and close your ears with your index finger. Turn your inner gaze towards the Ajna and breathe in through your nose. When you exhale, make a humming sound like a bee. Keep at it for about five minutes.

In Balance, Too Much, or Not Enough?

You have done this before, but you have to do it one more time. Bring those questions to the table and ask yourself if there are signs you noticed that have convinced you of possible blockages in the sixth chakra.

In Balance

Here are surefire signs that your Ajna has balanced energies.

Do I trust my intuition?

If you listen to your gut and it never betrays you, I have amazing news! Your third eye is open, and you know how to use your intuition correctly. Contrarily, if your gut is always wrong, it doesn't mean you don't have the power. You aren't receiving the right signals from your third eye.

Am I imaginative?

Is your imagination colorful? Chances are your third eye is open wide if you have a vivid imagination. Looking beyond the present situation requires imagination. If you aren't imaginative, you could work towards developing the quality! First, you have to remove the blockages, of course.

Can You Predict the Future?

Even if a vague power of clairvoyance exists in you, it's a good sign. Since this is not seen in most people, not having clairvoyance doesn't immediately mean your third eye is blocked. With more focus and meditation techniques, you could get there soon!

Too Much

Concentration of energies in the third eye can manifest in the following ways:

Overactive Mind

You'll be hallucinating or seeing visions. Nightmares are quite common too. You can compare this state to a sugar rush or caffeine overdose.

Insomnia

As your mind is hyperactive, you'll have trouble getting a good night's sleep. Prolonged lack of sleep can turn this into a chronic condition so it's time to fix the problem.

Not Enough

A lack of energies in the third eye has the following effects:

Memory Loss

Failure to remember events of the past and getting confused about the immediate past are symptoms of blockages in the third eye.

Lack of Concentration

The third eye specializes in focus, so when it lacks power, you won't be able to concentrate or remain focused on your job. This will in turn lead to procrastination and indecision.

Foods for the Third Eye Chakra

Purple vegetables and fruits are ideal for the Ajna. Eggplants, blueberries, purple cabbage, purple Kale, and purple grapes are examples. If you incorporate cacao into your diet it will act as a bonus because it's a serotonin-boosting food that relieves stress.

Crystals and Gems

Below are the gems that you should use for rituals and meditation sessions. Most of them are purple but some are bluish.

Amethyst: Deep purple in color, this gem brings awareness and strengthens intuition.

Lapis Lazuli: although this gem is used for the throat chakra, it also helps with the third eye because it helps you hone your psychic abilities, strengthens intuition, and increases spiritual awareness.

Sapphire: This stone can be purple or dark blue. It mainly helps with self-awareness and intuitive thinking.

Sodalite: The crystal is blue with white veins and acts as a source of focus during meditation

Angelite: It can be blue or gray, light pink, or brownish. The crystal helps with astral projection, boosts intuition, and relieves stress.

Key Takeaways

Let's look back at the top points of this chapter.

- The third eye is your intuition, and you need it for a better Perception of reality and what exists beyond it.

- Blockages manifest as headaches, sinuses, and insomnia. From a mental health perspective, you won't be able to imagine a bright future ahead of your present problems.

- Since the sixth chakra holds the key to inner knowledge and true wisdom, you should focus on it to know the truth about your other chakras as well.

All that remains now is to learn about the chakra at the top!

Chapter 9:

Crown Chakra—Sahasrara

At the helm of all other chakras, the crown chakra takes its regal position. Not only does it control the chakra system, but it affects the functions of your brain and nervous system. The chakra healing process culminates in the opening of the crown chakra. You can't possibly attain enlightenment without the help of the Sahasrara because it's the ultimate connection between life and spirituality.

You need to open the crown chakra to understand your purpose in life and your role in spiritual awakening. People who have an open crown chakra are usually happy and at peace. Blockages can make you skeptical, narrow-minded, and stubborn. Unless there is balance in the energies of the seventh chakra, complete healing is not possible.

An Introduction to the Crown Chakra

Below are the salient features of this chakra. As you read them, observe the connection with the lower chakras.

Location

The Sahasrara is located at the very top of your head. As the location suggests, the crown chakra is at its peak.

Meaning

This chakra has multiple meanings. Most people assume it has to be about spirituality, but it also has a link to bodily health and prosperity. To put it differently, the crown chakra brings awareness about your body and mind. It focuses on both inner and outer beauty, taking you on a journey toward happiness and well-being.

Mantra

SHAM is the mantra for the Sahasrara. Translating to "I am a vessel of love and light", the mantra truly encapsulates the essence of this chakra. It's as if the mantra exudes an aura of positivity.

Color

Violet and white are the colors associated with the crown chakra. White stands for purity and spiritual wisdom whereas violet represents the violet flame of transmutation. This flame is a combination of white and violet; always ablaze, the flame asserts the eternal quality of your soul. Life might be ephemeral but your soul travels to other dimensions.

Element

Divine consciousness is the element assigned to this chakra. From a spiritual perspective, everything merges with the divine consciousness at some point. So, the crown chakra contains energies that take you toward this omnipresence.

A Brief Overview of the Crown Chakra

The Sahasrara, meaning infinite, is the point of confluence of all the Nadis. It has an incredible amount of energy and the power it contains is capable of dispelling darkness with eternal light. Since it's pure light, many philosophies think of it as colorless and the seat of all qualities.

A lotus with thousands of petals is the symbol for this chakra. Representing the entirety of consciousness, the thousand petals signify completeness. As the ultimate goal of yoga is self-realization and understanding of the concept of divinity, the crown chakra is said to yield the most power. A meditative session on the chakras ends with a focus on the crown chakra when the Yogi has reached the climactic point or Nirvikalpa Samadhi (the highest form of concentration). To truly heal, you need to balance the energies in this chakra because blockages here can damage the system.

Imbalances in the Crown Chakra

An imbalanced crown chakra would mean chaos in the chakra system because it ensures the smooth flow of energy through the body and mind. While the physical signs of imbalance are related to balance and coordination, it can affect your personality as a whole.

Physical Signs

Below are some of the physical symptoms.

Poor Coordination

You might fall down often or have trouble maintaining balance. Maybe if you've started doing the previously mentioned yoga poses and think you're not able to do any of the poses perfectly, the issue might be with your crown chakra.

Poor Overall Health

A person whose crown chakra is out of balance suffers from frequent episodes of illnesses. Their physical functions are affected to a great extent, so it's natural they lack enthusiasm.

Mental Health Signs

From a mental health perspective, an open crown chakra enables you to take focus away from yourself. You'll be considering the world around you with a keen interest. But imbalances result in a warped worldview or selfishness. Here are some other signs.

Confusion

While this is also a sign of misdirected flow of energy to the third eye, crown chakra blockage also leads to confusion. You might have trouble understanding basic concepts, fail to read people, and end up in tricky situations when the Sahasrara is blocked.

Hyper Spiritualization

An over-emphasis on spirituality disconnects you from the world. That's not what you want. For your happiness, you need balance—an outlook that considers both the world we see and the one we can't physically perceive.

Poor Mental Health

Since the crown chakra is the culmination of all the other chakras, any problem here will throw your life into a mental health crisis. You'll be anxious or even depressed, you'll feel defeated and apathetic. Until the chakra is aligned, you won't be able to heal in a lasting way.

Why You Should Align the Crown Chakra

Without alignment of the energies in the seventh chakra, all efforts to achieve chakra healing will be rendered useless. Your physical and mental health will continue to suffer, and your personality will not be appealing to most people.

Removing Blockages

Meditation, pranayama, and asanas will help you remove blockages from this chakra. But before we delve into that, you should think carefully about the crown chakra and its unique functions. Some people believe the goals are unattainable because it's only something for gurus or fully dedicated yogis. That's not true at all. Maybe complete dedication will help you get that much closer to enlightenment, but healthy practices and a regular meditation routine will also go a long way in aligning the chakra.

Pranayama

Two breathwork exercises are necessary to remove blockages.

Nadi Sodhana

This is another name for alternate nostril breathing. It helps establish balance between the two hemispheres of the body and relieves stress. Removing toxins from the body also has a purifying effect. Here's what you have to do to perform this pranayama:

Sit comfortably and make sure your spine is straight. Bring your right hand in front of your face. Your fingers will be doing most of the job here. While the middle finger and index finger hold your forehead in place, the thumb and ring finger will close your nostrils. Close your eyes and take a few deep breaths. Then close your right nostril with your right thumb and breathe in through the left nostril. Following this, close the left nostril and breathe out through the right. Continue alternating for five to seven cycles (Eisler, 2015).

Kapalbhati

This pranayama helps with core strength, muscle growth, and improvement of overall physical health. Additionally, it increases focus, so it's essential for developing a meditation routine. To practice this breathwork exercise, you have to sit comfortably but make sure your back is erect. Breathe in slowly, relaxing your ab muscles. Then breathe out forcefully after contracting the ab muscles. Exhalation should be rapid for best results.

Asanas

Three asanas are particularly helpful for removing blockages in the crown chakra.

Headstand

Salamba Sirasana or the headstand is an intimidating yoga pose. Many seek to perfect this posture, many fail at it, and others are too afraid to try it out. The truth is, if you keep practicing, you'll be able to perform the headstand well and there's an alternative method for beginners. The pose is called the "King of all poses" because it has a huge amount of benefits.

Start the pose by going down on all fours. Intertwine your fingers, place them on the ground along with your forearm, and line up your elbows with your shoulders. Let your fingers hold the back of your head when you bring it down on the ground. Remain in this posture for a while. When you are able, you can lift your legs toward the ceiling. The modified pose doesn't include lifting your legs.

You can leave it to the headstand to give you all the qualities of each chakra. It strengthens the upper body and core, aids digestion, reduces stress, cures depression, and helps you focus.

Downward Dog

A favorite exercise even for people who don't practice yoga, the downward dog or adho mukha svanasana is a great stretching technique. Standing with your legs closed. From this position, slowly crawl forward until your buttocks face the ceiling. Breathe in and out steadily. Remain in the posture for as long as you are comfortable. Chronic back pain is significantly relieved by this posture. It also increases blood flow to the brain.

Fish Pose

The matsyasana or fish Pose will increase your lung capacity and help you breathe deeper. So, for your pranayama exercises, you'll need to practice this yoga pose. Fairly simple, the pose requires you to start in a seated position on the mat with your legs extended in front of you. Bring your hands under your lower body. Lean into your forearm after bending your elbows. Your chest should be facing the ceiling.

In Balance, Too Much, or Not Enough

What are the signs that will assure you about a balance of energies in this chakra? You know what to do, ask yourself those vital questions.

In Balance

Your questionnaire will consist of the following:

Am I self-aware?

This is just asking yourself how much you know about you! Do you think there are missing people, or do you fail to define yourself? It could mean the Sahasrara is out of balance.

Can I trust my inner compass?

A question that comes down to trusting yourself, it also brings intuition into play. If your third eye chakra is aligned, you might answer with a yes but that won't be a certain answer. You need to have full faith in yourself for assurance that the crown chakra is in alignment.

Too Much

Below are some personality traits that suggest there is too much energy concentrated on the seventh chakra.

Materialism

If you are too attached to material possessions, you haven't ascended to the level of spiritual development that's required for a balanced crown chakra.

Rigid Self-Identity

This means you aren't flexible. You stick to a certain identity you have given yourself and feel that you can't change it.

Not Enough

The following suggests a dearth of energy in the Sahasrara.

Depression and anxiety

Any signs of mental health issues should be a reminder that your chakras don't have the right amount of energy. When your crown chakra has blockages, you feel anxious and depressed because you get disconnected from your inner wisdom.

Lack of Compassion

To feel compassion, your heart chakra must be open. But even if the heart chakra has a balanced flow of energies, you still need help from the crown chakra to develop compassion.

Foods for the Crown Chakra

Detoxification is a goal of the crown chakra. So, fasting methods and detox diets are recommended for the Sahasrara.

Crystals and Gems

Meditation for the opening of the crown chakra relies on purification. So, the crystals used are either white or violet because these colors vibrate with the chakra.

Quartz: Almost transparent, this gem helps develop a focus for meditation. It absorbs negative energy and gives out positive vibes.

Selenite: Usually gray-white, Selenite assists any form of spiritual work.

Amethyst: This is a crystal used for both the crown chakra and the third eye chakra. It's purple in color and fosters spiritual awareness.

Tanzanite: A gem that helps expand your consciousness, Tanzanite is blue and also assists in the manifestation of wealth and prosperity.

Key Takeaways

The most important highlights of this chapter can be summarized in a few points:

- The crown chakra is truly at the top and ensures all the other chakras are in order.

- It makes spiritual development possible and helps you reach the universal consciousness.

- A culminating point for the chakras, the Sahasrara controls general health and mental peace.

- Breathwork and asanas are vital for removing blockages in this chakra.

You are now equipped with knowledge about the chakras. It's time to see how you can perform rituals incorporating all of them.

Chapter 10:

Chakra Balancing Rituals

You are now familiar with the steps to balance each chakra and stay in tune with the energy centers. Often, maintaining a healthy flow of energy isn't possible through balancing rituals of one specific chakra. Let's say you can't quite figure out what exactly is wrong with you. Although you've come to the realization that something is amiss, you can't point to it. In this case, overall chakra balancing rituals are a great help. When you perform one of these rituals, you could become aware of your problem.

Five Ways To Balance Your Chakras

I'll start with this brief discussion about five techniques to balance the flow of energy in your chakras. If you are a beginner, you can start here. Even if you have previously practiced rituals, going back to one of these methods is still beneficial. In fact, you should include them in your healing process for optimal benefits.

Visualization

You might have heard about creative visualization. Simply put, it's creating a mental image of your future—picturing your ideal self living the best life. For Chakra healing, visualization isn't the same. Instead of picturing your future, you have to concentrate on your present, the moment when you're meditating. Imagine energy flowing through your body—moving out of chakras that have an excess and entering the centers that are lacking. According to energy healer and Reiki practitioner Paritah Shah, a person feels a tingling sensation in certain parts of their body when they practice visualization. It's also possible for you to see colors (Estrada, 2021). Don't worry, it's a good sign as it means energy levels are being modified.

I believe it's best if you create a serene environment for your meditation. Being in natural surroundings is a major plus but you can also choose a quiet room. Some people prefer to listen to calming music while others like the sound of silence. Your preferences are important because not paying heed to them will have an impact on results. Sit still for a while and take a few deep breaths. Free your mind from worries about the future and don't dwell on past regrets. I say this because when we're alone in a quiet environment, chances are we'll think about what went wrong in the past or feel apprehensive about the future. Try your best to stay in the moment. Observe your breathing pattern and concentrate on your chakras. As you imagine energy flowing in and out of each chakra, those centers will give you a signal, usually in the form of a tingling sensation.

Reconnect With Nature

I can't emphasize this enough—nature is your friend in this healing journey. Snuggling in the nurturing arms of nature will help you overcome your illnesses and ease your troubles. I get that it might not be easy for you to take time out of your busy schedule to go hiking on a forest trail or take a walk on the beach. But no matter where you are, nature is always near you. Go ahead and explore its power! Here are a few suggestions.

- Meet your friends at a park or a garden instead of going to a cafe. Sharing quality time with loved ones in the midst of nature is a perfect way to tune into a peaceful state of mind.

- Visit a spot of natural beauty near you. You don't have to travel thousands of miles. I'm sure there is a place nearby that you can visit on the weekend. You can also go awe-walking when you follow a trail leading to a place with a spectacular view. It's believed that awe-walks increase mindfulness and facilitate meditation.

- If the previous point isn't an option for you, don't worry. Catching rays on your terrace or enjoying the views of a rainy afternoon can do wonders for you. Watch the birds, hear the sound of rustling leaves, or feel the warmth of the sun—do whatever you can to establish a bond with nature.

- Sometimes looking at pictures of natural landscapes has a soothing effect on us. When you meditate you can look at beautiful pictures of nature in its pristine glory.

Sound Healing

Sound baths have been used as a healing practice since ancient times. Each chakra relates to some specific sound frequencies. The vibrations created by sound waves can help change the flow of energies and remove blockages. A study conducted in 2016 shows that the 62 participants exposed to sound healing through the singing bowl experienced less anxiety and fatigue (Goldsby et al., 2016).

By shifting our brainwaves through the process of entertainment, sound waves help in changing the state of our minds (Martinez, 2021). "Entrainment" refers to a procedure that synchronizes our brain waves to one stable frequency (Martinez, 2021). Rhythm and frequency regulate the brain waves so our mind can shift from the beta state (normal waking consciousness) to the alpha state (relaxed consciousness). It's also possible to shift to the theta or the meditative state and the delta state which is equivalent to sleep. Healing can occur when you listen to certain sound frequencies while you sleep.

Sound healing requires you to be both active and passive for optimal results. When you're lying down or relaxing, you're allowing yourself to be passive for sound healing to occur. By chanting mantras, performing breathing exercises, and through vocal toning, you can remain active even while you let your body relax. Vocal toning is especially helpful because it enables you to fully tune the frequencies of your body.

Practice Chakra-Balancing Chants

Every chakra has a special mantra or chant as you've seen in the earlier chapters. They have unique meanings relating to the chakra they're assigned. When you chant these mantras, the energies in your body are redirected to where they belong. You might be wondering how exactly you should practice the chants. I believe the best way is to keep chanting the mantra throughout your meditation. Try thinking about the chakra and all its associations when you breathe in and chant the mantra when you exhale.

Do a Chakra Color Meditation

Colors have a frequency that aligns with energy flow to your chakras. I have introduced you to the concept of color meditation for each chakra, but what if you don't know which chakra you should meditate on? Well, in that case, you can meditate by visualizing all the colors in order of where they are located in the spinal column, starting from red denoting the root chakra, and ending in purple or white denoting the crown chakra. As you visualize the color simply through imagination or by looking at a gem or crystal, reflect on the function of that chakra. For example, when you're visualizing red, think about grounding and self-confidence.

Applying the Concept of Chakras to Feng Shui

Chakra healing is for your body and mind, but the same concept works for your home. Feng Shui, which is concerned with balancing the energy flow in your home, uses pretty much the same methodology. You'd want your home to be vibrating with energies that are in tune with the environment—that's the aim of Feng Shui. Just like each chakra is situated in a certain area of the body and has a meaning that corresponds to health and wellness, each corner of the house is associated with an aspect of life. Let's look at the Feng Shui equivalents of chakras for a better understanding of this concept.

The root chakra in Feng Shui would be the family and health area. We consider the middle of the home and the area slightly left to it as the center of good health and happy relationships. Strong roots and family ties help in your growth as a person. It's important to keep items depicting your family history like photographs and heirlooms.

In Feng Shui, the far-left corner of the home is connected to wealth and prosperity. We can think of it as the equivalent of our sacral chakra. It's the place where we feel power as well as fear and gratitude. Balancing the energies here is extremely necessary for financial security and abundance. While money makes us powerful, it should also keep us humble and thankful for opportunities. Keeping that in mind, you should place items expressing gratitude.

The far middle area of the house symbolizes fame and reputation. Self–worth and confidence exudes from this area, so it's often compared to the solar plexus chakra. Animal prints and candles help in balancing the energies here. You'll know something is wrong when you don't feel empowered and confident about yourself while at home.

Energies contributing to thriving relationships are located at the far-right corner of the house. In the chakra system, the heart chakra has a similar connotation. The heart nurtures our body and helps us feel love for others. Likewise, this corner of the house should have positive energies that improve relationships. To activate the energies here and remove blockages, keep items in multiples of two, and don't forget to place items symbolic of love.

Children remind us of creativity and imagination. The middle right area of the house is dedicated to creativity and is often associated with children. It inspires us to explore our inner child and find our inner voice. As it concerns itself with seeking guidance from the inner voice, it's seen as the equivalent of the throat chakra. Metallic and round items help remove blockages from this area.

The third-eye chakra is similar to the helpful people and travel area which is located in the inside right corner of the house. Just as the energies in the third-eye chakra provide inner vision and spirituality, the Feng Shui concept deems the inside right area to be a place for upliftment and connection with the spiritual realm. This area should be a place of worship or space for meditation.

Career and prosperity are associated with the inside center. The energies here correspond to the energies in our crown chakra. We discover our true path in life and understand our capabilities through the energies located here. Water is best for activating this area.

The Twelve-Step Chakra Self-Healing Ritual

Crystals and gems are used in chakra healing practices and you're now aware of crystals connected to each chakra. But like I said at the beginning of this chapter, you might not be sure about energy imbalances. Perform the following ritual for complete healing.

1. Collect gems and crystals for each chakra. You should have more than one for each because later you'll get to choose which you are attracted to the most.

2. Cleanse them in cold water and half-cup sea salt. Keep a bowl of cold water ready in case you need to cleanse them again later.

3. Select crystals that appeal to you most but be sure to include stones for each chakra.

4. Charge the crystals by holding them one at a time and spelling out your intention for choosing them. For example, you can say

"I want to find my grounding" for the crystals symbolizing your root chakra.

5. In a place where you're comfortable, lay down and relax. Play your favorite meditation music and burn some incense or light a few scented candles. Place the crystals according to their position on the spinal column.

6. Once the crystals are in place, breathe in and out focusing on each chakra. This is similar to the breathwork you practice for separate chakras; the only difference is you don't stop after one is complete. You can also chant the mantra for each chakra.

7. Take in the calmness around you. Feel the energies entering your body and think about the positive things that are going to happen.

8. Express your gratitude for what you already have and the gifts you're about to receive.

9. Visualize a better future for yourself and the earth.

10. The ceremony is now over so it's time to get up. Don't rush into it and sit up straight suddenly. Gently remove the stones from your body and wash them in the water bowl you'd kept near you. Touch the water for self-purification and sprinkle some of it on the chakra center.

11. Do a stretching exercise or yoga to help your body transition to its regular state.

12. Perform a sacred bath to end the ritual. This bath contains herbs, and you can also decorate your tub with plants, crystals, and sea shells.

With that, your ritual will be completed. Usually performed at the point of the moon's transition from the sign of Aries to the star of Ashwini, it can be repeated in each moon cycle.

Key Takeaways

Let's remind ourselves of some of the highlights of this chapter.

- If you aren't sure where to begin or which chakra to focus on, meditate on the colors and mantras of each chakra. After a while, you'll realize where the imbalance is located.

- Spend time in the company of nature. Simply looking at stunning views can help you relieve some stress.

- Sound baths are therapeutic because by tuning your energies you can reach a meditative state.

- Feng Shui is quite similar to the chakra system, only its principles are applicable to your home. But you need to balance the energies in your home too. So, why not practice both?

- A twelve-step Ayurvedic healing process with gems and crystals cleanses your body and mind, rejuvenating you completely.

- Always begin a ritual with a positive mindset and don't forget to use fragrances and meditation music for relaxation.

Even after learning about the healing powers of your seven chakras, you could have some doubts because you haven't seen medical science back it up. In the next chapter, you're going to find out how modern scientific studies prove the efficacy of ancient healing practices.

Chapter 11:

Emerging Scientific Studies

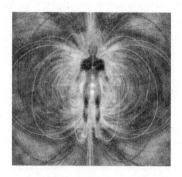

A very common argument or retort against alternative medicine is a snarky comment about how science doesn't provide any evidence for such therapies and practices. We are mostly dependent on scientific research and so we wait for studies to show if a certain healing procedure is worth undergoing. Some people boldly claim that they don't care for proof and they're willing to try something new based on testimonies. Well, that's completely fine, but if you aren't one of them, don't feel guilty. It's okay to have doubts and curiosity is essential for discoveries. Also, I have great news! Studies have indeed revealed the effectiveness of chakra healing and you'll see how. Two main branches of research have delved into this topic—biofield science and epigenetics. Let's see what they have to say.

Biofield Science

A name that you must know in this context is the name of Dr. Richard Hammerschlag, Ph.D. He's a renowned neuroscientist who recently co-founded the Consciousness and Healing Initiative (CHI). An organization consisting of scientists, educators, health practitioners, innovators, and artists, CHI aims to promote transdisciplinary science and real-world application of consciousness and healing techniques (Nova Institute, 2016). Dr. Hammerschlag reviews studies related to the science of consciousness and specifically biofield practices.

I realize you're eager to know what biofield science means, so here is a brief explanation: Biofields are generated from different parts of the body, mainly the brain (EEG) and the heart (ECG). These biofields are electromagnetic patterns that can be manipulated for healing purposes. Therapies based on biofields were popular in ancient Chinese and Ayurvedic medicine. Notice how similar it is to the chakra system. Each chakra emanates waves of energy, and we practice balancing rituals to control the flow of this energy.

Dr. Hammerschlag researched the physiological implications and came up with positive results. He was supported by the Nova Institute and his peers working there. At a conference organized by Dr. Hammerschlag, researchers shared published papers on biofield science, and the brilliant results obtained from related practices. We can consider this a movement that sent ripples through the community of people interested in alternative medicine.

Biofield Therapies

So, what exactly are biofield therapies? You might be thinking that all healing therapies based on ancient techniques have been able to secure a place within the realm of biofield science, but that would be a stretch. Biofield science concerns itself with the subtle energy system surrounding our body. There are three major energy channels—meridians, chakras, and the biofield. Meridians are lines of energy present in our bodies. Practices such as acupuncture use the meridians as an important component. Chakras are energy centers as you've learned. The biofield is energy emanating from our body and extends up to eight feet. Some healers can see colors or shapes in the biofield, but mostly, it's felt by hand. Normally, you'd have to lie down on a massage table while the healer assesses your biofield. People can choose to heal existing problems or prevent future issues. Reiki, healing touch, and therapeutic touch are the most common biofield therapies. Remember that the client's best intentions are always kept in mind in these therapies.

Reiki

Popularized by Mikao Usui in 1900s Japan, Reiki is a healing method that uses universal energy to mitigate problems with physical or mental health for overall well-being. The healer invites their client to open themselves to the energy surrounding them. Gradually, through hand gestures corresponding to energy centers, imbalances are rectified. Some people wrongly assume that Reiki has ties with a religion or specific school of thought. In reality, it's completely independent of religion and anyone can participate in a healing session. According to reports, Reiki has helped in relieving stress and anxiety after hospital procedures (Berger and Thompson, 2019).

Healing Touch

Janet Mentgen, a nurse by profession, introduced the concept of Healing Touch in 1989. It became quite popular in the US and people still opt for it because of its simple approach. Unlike Reiki, Healing Touch focuses on specific hand gestures to figure out imbalances in energy before beginning the process. While Reiki is more generalized, this method is controlled and structured. The basic principle, however, remains the same—to seek the ultimate well-being of the client. Trauma patients have benefited from Healing Touch, as studies show that the practice helps reduce pain and anxiety (Berger and Thompson, 2019).

Therapeutic Touch

This practice was founded by Dolores Krieger and Dora Kunz in the 1970s. A method similar to Healing Touch, it was later replaced by HT to a large extent. But we shouldn't underestimate its significance as people in the US started to get more curious about biofield therapies when they learned about Therapeutic Touch.

Pranic Healing

Pranic healing isn't very different from chakra healing. Gems and crystals are used in this practice to remove blockages in chakras and restore positive energies. However, this method also considers the biofield as a major component that isn't deemed essential for all forms of chakra healing. A parallel can be drawn between pranic healing and the 114-chakra system introduced by Dr. Amit Ray as it stresses the importance of a network of Nadis channeling energy to various parts of the body (Chapter 1).

Epigenetics

Epigenetics is the science that studies the role of behavior and environment on your genes. Your genes influence your health, everyone knows that. For years, there's been a tussle between two groups of researchers—one claiming that genetics have the most impact while the other argues that the environment's impact is greater. Well, it's now been revealed through epigenetics that behavior and the outside environment can direct your genes to turn "on" and "off", meaning whether they are activated or not depends on external factors. Genetic changes affect the type of protein secreted in the genes, but epigenetics decides how your body will react to these proteins. One crucial difference between epigenetic changes and genetic mutations is that the former is reversible (CDC, 2020).

Why am I talking about epigenetics in connection with chakra healing and alternative medicine? For one, from epigenetics-related research, it's now evident that the environment we are in can affect our genes, so we can safely say that the energies surrounding us can influence our bodies in a way we might not have imagined decades ago. Before we go into a more in-depth analysis of chakras and epigenetics, let's find out how epigenetics works.

How It Works

Epigenetics functions through the following processes:

DNA Methylation

When a chemical compound is added to the DNA to block proteins that decide how a gene reads, methylation occurs. This can be undone through demethylation by removing the chemical compound.

Histone Modification

Histone is a protein that wraps the DNA. Sometimes they are tightly packed, and this stops proteins from accessing the DNA and it's turned "off". On the other hand, when histones are loosely packed, the proteins access the DNA, and genes turn "on".

Non-Coding RNA

DNA is responsible for the formation of coding and non-coding RNA. Coding RNA makes proteins and non-coding RNA blocks the proteins, therefore changing gene expression. It's also possible for non-coding RNA to modify histones.

How Epigenetics Change

Changes in epigenetics are not sudden. They take place over a period of time and depend on several factors. Here are some important points about epigenetic changes:

Epigenetics and Development

Throughout your life, your cells undergo changes. Even before you are born, epigenetics are in action, determining the function of cells. Initially, cells have the same gene. As you mature, the cells get assigned a particular function. For example, nerve cells help transmit information whereas muscle cells facilitate movement.

Epigenetics and Age

Aging affects epigenetics and changes continue to happen throughout your life. A study was conducted on people of different age groups, and it revealed that DNA methylation decreases with age. We've seen how DNA methylation is an important part of epigenetics, so this proves that epigenetics is a continuing process (Heyn et al., 2012).

Epigenetics and Reversibility

While some epigenetic changes are permanent, others can be reversed. An example of this is how DNA methylation works in smokers and non-smokers. In smokers, DNA methylation is reduced but when they quit smoking, there's a significant increase (MacCartney et al., 2018).

How Epigenetics Impact Health

From the previous section, it becomes clear that epigenetic changes play a pivotal role in your body. Therefore, it's no surprise that your health is intrinsically related to these changes. Below is a discussion about the effects of epigenetics on health. To later find a connection between chakra healing and epigenetics, we must look into the implications of epigenetics on the body and mind.

Infections

When a body is non-alkaline or acidic, often resulting from your diet or interstitial fluid, it may cause pathogens to weaken your immune system. One way in which they do this is by tweaking the epigenetic makeup of cells. For example, the diseased state known as mycobacterium tuberculosis can turn off the IL-12B gene that's responsible for immunity.

Cancer

Genetic mutations often heighten the risk of cancer. Genes that are at maximum risk are the Breast Cancer 1 (BRCA1) and Breast Cancer 2 (BRCA2) genes. A person has two copies of BRCA1 and BRCA2 genes, one from the father and the other from the mother. Mutation of one of these genes won't lead to any significant impact, but when the second copy undergoes mutation, there remains no BRCA1 or BRCA2 gene that functions normally in the body. This is when the person develops cancer (CDC, 2022). The second mutation is only present in the cancer tissue. Epigenetic changes happening in your cells, particularly with regard to DNA methylation, can determine whether you're at risk. Any mutation in the BRCA1 gene exposes you to cancer because there's a chance this is the second mutation as discussed above. Research has found that DNA methylation can turn the BRCA1 gene expression "off" and this is a primary cause of breast cancer (Tang et al., 2016).

Nutrition During Pregnancy

How a pregnant woman behaves during pregnancy and the environment she is in are factors that determine the health of the baby. Nutrition is the most consequential element in this regard. We are aware that consumption of alcohol can seriously affect the baby but other foods or the lack of proper nutrition could also modify the epigenetics of the child. In the winter of 1944-1945, the Netherlands suffered through a famine that inadvertently also caused health problems in children whose mothers were pregnant with them at the time. They were later found to be at risk of developing heart disease, Type 2 diabetes, and schizophrenia (Heijmans et al., 2008). Their epigenetics were different from their siblings due to increased and decreased DNA methylation in certain cells.

I believe you are now able to recognize the importance of epigenetics and the truth must have hit home by now—yes, I'm talking about the fact that you can actually modify your genetics through behavior and the surrounding environment. Dr. Bruce Lipton speaks about shocking information that doesn't get mentioned due to the dominant narrative surrounding traditional medicine. In fact, "A minimum of one-third of all medical intervention is a placebo effect. That's the result of positive thinking", says Dr. Lipton. For example, Statin, a type of medication used to prevent cardiovascular diseases, is said to only help about 3% of the people who take it and cause dangerous side effects for 23% of them (Boyd, 2018). Now think about this—if your behavior has an enormous effect on genes, changing your behavior for the better will mean getting healthier even from a genetic perspective. This impact is greater than that of some medications. Epigenetic changes don't only affect the child if their mother is exposed to stress, environmental factors, or poor nutrition, but multiple future generations might also carry the mutations through a process called transgenerational inheritance (NIEH, 2022).

Epigenetics and Chakra Healing

From the conclusions drawn by Dr. Lipton, we can say that the methods of Biofield science could possibly be game-changing for anybody looking to improve their health. Chakra healing takes into consideration environmental factors as well as behavioral modifications. Essentially, you are forcing some genes to turn off and others to turn on by regulating your energies. Changing your lifestyle to accommodate your health should always be a priority and you already know how that's good for you. But this is more than just adapting to a better lifestyle—it's about neuroplasticity.

Trust me, the concept of neuroplasticity is pretty simple—it's about forming new neural pathways in the brain as a consequence of changes in emotions, way of thinking, present situation, and external environment (Erikson, 2015). Some examples will make this easier for you to understand.

- Brain functions of stroke victims go through severe transformations, so new neural pathways are created for them to be able to function.

- Normally, a person isn't able to see underwater, but deep-sea divers can see better than most others because they control their eye lenses and pupils in a different way by training their brains.

- To play a musical instrument, one has to develop more focus than the average person. As a result of their training, gray matter is built in areas of the brain that help with playing the instruments.

- Athletes' brains are also stimulated when they perform and hence changes are noticeable within years of starting athletic practice.

- Meditation improves brain activity, but permanent changes are visible in the brains of Tibetan monks who meditate regularly. This goes on to suggest that the benefits of meditation last beyond the time when you meditate.

From the above examples, it's clear that the positive impact of chakra healing too is long-lasting. Suppose you are balancing the energies in your root chakra, the steps you take to strengthen your foundation will be recorded by your brain. Thoughts don't usually flow in a linear pattern, but you can direct them through chakra healing. It's definitely possible to forge physical improvements by controlling energy flow in your body and mind. To live well, your stress levels need to be low, and once your energies are in tune, you will experience less stress. Not to mention, reduced stress impacts both physical and mental health, helping you be happier and feel better about your life.

When you implement all the tips and suggestions I shared in the book, you'll be tweaking your brain functions to gradually manifest a visible transformation. I understand you might be curious to learn more about the scientific side of chakra healing and my third book *Guide to Healing the Human Biofield through Integrative Medicine and Health: Discovering the Science behind Energy Healing, Integrating Complementary and Alternative Medicine Therapies, Transforming Health and Wellness* will be highlighting this topic.

Key Takeaways

Let's go over the main connections between science and chakra healing:

- Biofield science is a branch of scientific studies that concerns itself with healing through the energy field surrounding our body.

- Several therapies have developed under the larger banner of biofield science. These include Reiki, Healing Touch, Therapeutic Touch, and Pranic Healing.

- Epigenetic theory, accepted by most researchers in the scientific world, has a link to chakra healing.

- By determining how much energy flows into your chakras, you are forcing your body and mind to change for the better.

So, you have almost reached the end of the book. Take a breather now just to appreciate yourself for reading about the chakras. You now have the key to opening up new possibilities and gifting yourself better health. Yes, when you practice chakra healing, you will be giving yourself the most wonderful gift on the planet—good health and persistent wellness. I'm not claiming that the road ahead is not bumpy at all. In every journey, you will encounter some setbacks and the process isn't different for chakra healing. Maybe you won't be able to meditate every day, or you won't find the crystals you're looking for. But imagine that at the end of this road is a beautiful garden where you can soak in the sun and feast your eyes on colorful flowers! Your future is indeed just as bright and amazing!

Conclusion

Reflect on your chakras or the energy centers in your body. With the information you now have, make notes about what you believe could be the anomaly in your chakra system. Of course, without performing a healing ritual, you won't be able to fully understand what's wrong, but a great way to get started is to simply ask yourself questions. You already have these questions in each chapter about the seven chakras, so you can have a look and notice how you're answering them. I believe you will arrive at a rough conclusion that can be verified through meditations and rituals.

Before I bring things to a close, I'd like to give you one last suggestion—give yourself time to heal. Don't rush into something because you think it's a shortcut. Chakra healing isn't a quick fix; it's for the long term. You might not see immediate results, but with time, you'll experience permanent changes. Next time you see that advert claiming to fast track your healing process, don't trust it. No one has as much power to improve your life as you do. There is no other miraculous trick than what you can do for your well-being.

Always remember that this power is within you; it's innate. External factors like medicines and supplements are not necessary to bolster it. What's more important is that you form a connection with your inner self and harness your healing power. Finding blockages in your chakras and removing them will open the path to wellness. You'll soon be on your way to living a harmonious life, perfectly in tune with universal energies.

You know what can hold you back? Constantly debating whether it's worth a try and delaying the journey. Start today because a happy future is waiting for you! I'd really love to know your thoughts on this book and also about your progress with chakra healing, so I'm asking you to please leave a review on Amazon. I'm sure others would be thrilled to hear more about your experience as well!

With that, there's only one thing left for me to say—I wish you all the best for your healing and hope you finally see the results you've been waiting to see!

References

Ayurveda Rituals. (n.d.). *12 Step Chakra Self-care Healing Ritual - Ayurveda Rituals Spa.* Ayurveda Rituals. https://ayurvedaritualsspa.com/12-step-chakra-self-care-healing-ritual/

Berger, C., & Thompson, S. (2009). *Biofield Therapies.* Www.counseling.org. https://www.counseling.org/news/aca-blogs/aca-counseling-corner/aca-member-blogs/2019/06/12/biofield-therapies

Boyd, D. (2018, October 16). *Dr. Bruce Lipton Shocked the World with his Discovery.* The American Institute of Stress. https://www.stress.org/dr-bruce-lipton-shocked-the-world-with-his-discovery

CDC. (2020, August 3). *What is Epigenetics?* Centers for Disease Control and Prevention. https://www.cdc.gov/genomics/disease/epigenetics.htm

Chopra, D. (2016, April 21). *3 Ways You Can Benefit from Your Chakras.* Chopra. https://chopra.com/articles/3-ways-you-can-benefit-from-your-chakras

Cronkleton, E. (2020, July 28). *Lion's Breath Benefits and How to Roar.* Healthline. https://www.healthline.com/health/practicing-lions-breath

Crystal Life. (2020, June 18). *Feng Shui and the Chakras | Crystal Life Technology, Inc.* Crystal Life. https://www.crystal-life.com/feng-shui-chakras/

Desy, P. L. (2019, May 9). *Find Out the Function and Purpose of Your Crown Chakra.* Learn Religions. https://www.learnreligions.com/crown-chakra-1724455

Eisler, M. (2015, November 4). *Nadi Shodhana: How to Practice Alternate Nostril Breathing.* Chopra. https://chopra.com/articles/nadi-shodhana-how-to-practice-alternate-nostril-breathing

Enlightened Energetics. (2015, March 21). *Neuroplasticity, Epigenetics, and Your Energy Body (or How We Change).* Mommy Mystic. https://mommymystic.wordpress.com/2015/03/21/neuroplasticity-epigenetics-and-your-energy-body-or-how-we-change/

Estrada, J. (2020, January 4). *Feeling out of sorts? Here's how to balance your chakras.* Well+Good. https://www.wellandgood.com/chakra-balancing/

Fernandez, C. (2018, October 2). *Here's What Happens During an Aura and Chakra Cleansing.* Oprah Daily. https://www.oprahdaily.com/life/health/a23508493/aura-chakra-cleansing/

Fondin, M. (2015a, January 15). *Your Third Chakra: Find Power & and Warrior Energy in Your Solar Plexus & Manipura Chakra.* Chopra. https://chopra.com/articles/your-third-chakra-find-power-and-warrior-energy-in-your-solar-plexus-manipura-chakra

Fondin, M. (2015b, May 26). *Trust Your Intuition With the Sixth Chakra.* Chopra. https://www.chopra.com/articles/trust-your-intuition-with-the-sixth-chakra

Fondin, M. (2018, March 23). *The Philosophy Behind the Chakras.* Chopra. https://chopra.com/articles/the-philosophy-behind-the-chakras

Fondin, M. (2020a, June 4). *Connect to the Divine With the Seventh Chakra.* Chopra. https://www.chopra.com/articles/connect-to-the-divine-with-the-seventh-chakra

Fondin, M. (2020b, October 7). *The Root Chakra: Muladhara*. Chopra. https://chopra.com/articles/the-root-chakra-muladhara

Gabriel, R. (2015, January 15). *How to Use Sound to Heal Yourself.* Chopra. https://chopra.com/articles/how-to-use-sound-to-heal-yourself?_gl=1

Goodnet Team. (2019). *Chakra Healing: How To Open Your Root Chakra*. Goodnet. https://www.goodnet.org/articles/root-chakra-healing-how-to-open-your

Greater Good in Action Staff. (n.d.). *Loving-Kindness Meditation (Greater Good in Action)*. Ggia.berkeley.edu. https://ggia.berkeley.edu/practice/loving_kindness_meditation

Heijmans, B. T., Tobi, E. W., Stein, A. D., Putter, H., Blauw, G. J., Susser, E. S., Slagboom, P. E., & Lumey, L. H. (2008). Persistent epigenetic differences associated with prenatal exposure to famine in humans. *Proceedings of the National Academy of Sciences, 105*(44), 17046–17049. https://doi.org/10.1073/pnas.0806560105

Heyn, H., Li, N., Ferreira, H. J., Moran, S., Pisano, D. G., Gomez, A., Diez, J., Sanchez-Mut, J. V., Setien, F., Carmona, F. J., Puca, A. A., Sayols, S., Pujana, M. A., Serra-Musach, J., Iglesias-Platas, I., Formiga, F., Fernandez, A. F., Fraga, M. F., Heath, S. C., & Valencia, A. (2012). Distinct DNA methylomes of newborns and centenarians. *Proceedings of the National Academy of Sciences of the United States of America, 109*(26), 10522–10527. https://doi.org/10.1073/pnas.1120658109

Indigo Wellness. (2013). *What is the origin of the chakra system? – Indigo Massage & Wellness*. Indigo Wellness. https://indigomassagetherapy.com/uncategorized/what-is-the-origin-of-the-chakra-system/

Isha Sadhguru. (n.d.). *Muladhara Chakra: Why It's The Most important Chakra*. Isha.sadhguru.org. Retrieved January 5, 2023, from https://isha.sadhguru.org/us/en/wisdom/article/muladhara-chakra

Jain, R. (2020, September 3). *Manipura Chakra: Healing Powers of Solar Plexus Chakra | Arhanta Blog*. Arhanta Yoga Ashram. https://www.arhantayoga.org/blog/manipura-chakra-healing-powers-of-the-solar-plexus-chakra/

Kafatos, M. C., Chevalier, G., Chopra, D., Hubacher, J., Kak, S., & Theise, N. D. (2015). Biofield Science: Current physics perspectives. *Global Advances in Health and Medicine, 4*(1_suppl), gahmj.2015.011. https://doi.org/10.7453/gahmj.2015.011.suppl

Laine, K. (2021, November 10). *Balance Your Chakras With Sound Therapy: Here's How*. YouAligned™. https://www.yogiapproved.com/sound-therapy-chakra-balancing/

Lechner, T. (2020, January 8). *Learn About Your Seven Chakras and How to Keep Them in Balance*. Chopra. https://chopra.com/articles/learn-about-your-seven-chakras-and-how-to-keep-them-in-balance

Martinez, N. (2021, October 3). *mindbodygreen*. Mindbodygreen. https://www.mindbodygreen.com/0-17515/what-you-need-to-know-about-sound-healing.html

McCartney, D. L., Stevenson, A. J., Hillary, R. F., Walker, R. M., Bermingham, M. L., Morris, S. W., Clarke, T.-K., Campbell, A., Murray, A. D., Whalley, H. C., Porteous, D. J., Visscher, P. M., McIntosh, A. M., Evans, K. L., Deary, I. J., & Marioni, R. E. (2018). Epigenetic signatures of starting and stopping smoking. *EBioMedicine, 37*, 214–220. https://doi.org/10.1016/j.ebiom.2018.10.051

National Institute of Environmental Health Sciences (NIEH). (2022). *Epigenetics*. National Institute of Environmental Health Sciences.

https://www.niehs.nih.gov/health/topics/science/epigenetics
/index.cfm#:~:text=Researchers%20unravel%20role%20of%2
0epigenetics%20in%20development%2C%20inheritance%2C

Neumann, K. D. (2022, June 14). *Your Complete Guide To The Body Chakras.* Forbes Health. https://www.forbes.com/health/body/body-chakras-guide/

Nova Institute. (2016, February 25). *Biofield Science and Healing: A New Chapter.* Nova Institute for Health. https://novainstituteforhealth.org/biofield-science-healing-a-new-chapter/

Onyx Team. (2020, May 3). *Root Chakra Healing: Everything you Need to Know | Onyx Integrative AZ.* Onyx Integrative Medicine & Aesthetics. https://onyxintegrative.com/root-chakra-healing/

Osa, B. (2021, August 7). *The 7 Healing Benefits of Chakra Alignment | Blue Osa.* Blue Osa Yoga Retreat + Spa. https://www.blueosa.com/the-7-healing-benefits-of-chakra-alignment-blue-osa/

Phutrakool, P., & Pongpirul, K. (2022). Acceptance and use of complementary and alternative medicine among medical specialists: a 15-year systematic review and data synthesis. *Systematic Reviews, 11*(1). https://doi.org/10.1186/s13643-021-01882-4

Quinn, J. (2021, December 15). *Feng Shui Is Like Chakra-Balancing For Your Home.* Sunday Edit. https://edit.sundayriley.com/fengshui-chakra-balancing-home/

Ray, D. A. (2017, November 22). *72000 Nadis and 114 Chakras in Human Body.* Amit Ray. https://amitray.com/72000-nadis-and-114-chakras-in-human-body/

Raypole, C. (2020, August 18). *Kundalini Meditation: Benefits, How To Try, and Dangers.* Healthline. https://www.healthline.com/health/kundalini-meditation

Shah, P. (2020, August 20). *The Chopra Center.* The Chopra Center. https://chopra.com/articles/what-is-a-chakra

Shah, P. (2022, June 6). *Meet the 7 Chakra Colors in a Guided Meditation for Healing.* Paritashahhealing.com. https://paritashahhealing.com/chakra-color-meditation-healing/

Snyder, S. (2021a, May 21). What You Need to Know About the Ajna Chakra. *Yoga Journal.* https://www.yogajournal.com/yoga-101/chakras-yoga-for-beginners/chakratuneup2015-intro-ajna/

Snyder, S. (2021b, August 18). *Everything You Need to Know About the Crown Chakra.* Yoga Journal. https://www.yogajournal.com/yoga-101/chakras-yoga-for-beginners/intro-sahasrara-crown-chakra/

Sovik, R. (n.d.). *Learn Kapalabhati (Skull Shining Breath).* Yogainternational.com. https://yogainternational.com/article/view/learn-kapalabhati-skull-shining-breath

Stelter, G. (2016, October 4). *A Beginner's Guide to the 7 Chakras and Their Meanings.* Healthline; Healthline Media. https://www.healthline.com/health/fitness-exercise/7-chakras

Tang, Q., Cheng, J., Cao, X., Surowy, H., & Burwinkel, B. (2016). Blood-based DNA methylation as biomarker for breast cancer: a systematic review. *Clinical Epigenetics, 8,* 115. https://doi.org/10.1186/s13148-016-0282-6

Tiffany. (2016, June 17). *Food and Chakra Pairing: Balancing and Healing Our Energy Centers Through Food.* Parsnips and Pastries. https://www.parsnipsandpastries.com/chakra-food-pairing-balancing-healing-energy-centers-food/

Tiny Rituals Blog. (n.d.). *Sacral Chakra Stones: 11 Stones That Make A Huge Difference.* Tiny Rituals. https://tinyrituals.co/blogs/tiny-rituals/sacral-chakra-stones

Tracey, J. (2020a, October 31). *Crown Chakra Stones | Top 7 Sahasrara Crystals.* 7 Chakra Store. https://7chakrastore.com/blogs/news/crown-chakra-stones

Tracey, J. (2020b, October 31). *Heart Chakra Stones | Top 7 Anahata Crystals.* 7 Chakra Store. https://7chakrastore.com/blogs/news/heart-chakra-stones

Tracey, J. (2020c, October 31). *Solar Plexus Chakra Stones | Top 7 Manipura Crystals.* 7 Chakra Store. https://7chakrastore.com/blogs/news/solar-plexus-chakra-stones

Tracey, J. (2020d, October 31). *Third Eye Chakra Stones | Top 7 Ajna Crystals.* 7 Chakra Store. https://7chakrastore.com/blogs/news/third-eye-chakra-stones

Tracy, J. (2020, August 31). *Root Chakra Stones | Top 7 Muladhara Crystals.* 7 Chakra Store. https://7chakrastore.com/blogs/news/root-chakra-stones

Villines, Z. (2022, May 24). *What are chakras? Concept, origins, and effect on health.* Www.medicalnewstoday.com. https://www.medicalnewstoday.com/articles/what-are-chakras-concept-origins-and-effect-on-health

Ward, T. (2015, July 23). *Visualize Your Way To Balanced Chakras- A Guided Meditation.* Sivana East. https://blog.sivanaspirit.com/balanced-chakras-meditation/

YJ Editors. (2007a, August 28). *Dolphin Pose.* Yoga Journal. https://www.yogajournal.com/poses/dolphin-pose-2/

YJ Editors. (2007b, August 28). *Eagle Pose.* Yoga Journal. https://www.yogajournal.com/poses/eagle-pose/

YJ Editors. (2021a, March 12). *Intro to the Fourth Chakra: Heart Chakra (Anahata) | Subtle Body.* Yoga Journal.

https://www.yogajournal.com/yoga-101/chakras-yoga-for-beginners/intro-heart-chakra-anahata/

YJ Editors. (2021b, April 27). *What You Need to Know About the Sacral Chakra*. Yoga Journal. https://www.yogajournal.com/yoga-101/chakras-yoga-for-beginners/intro-sacral-chakra-svadhisthana/

YJ Editors. (2021c, June 15). *Everything You Need to Know About the Navel Chakra*. Yoga Journal. https://www.yogajournal.com/yoga-101/chakras-yoga-for-beginners/intro-third-navel-chakra/

YJ Editors. (2021d, July 30). *Everything You Need to Know About the Throat Chakra*. Yoga Journal. https://www.yogajournal.com/yoga-101/chakras-yoga-for-beginners/chakratuneup2015-intro-visuddha/

Yoga In Daily Life. (n.d.). *Vishuddhi Chakra*. Www.yogaindailylife.org. Retrieved January 8, 2023, from https://www.yogaindailylife.org/system/en/chakras/vishuddhi-chakra

Yoga in Daily Life. (n.d.-a). *Manipura Chakra*. Www.yogaindailylife.org. Retrieved January 8, 2023, from https://www.yogaindailylife.org/system/en/chakras/manipura-chakra

Yoga in Daily Life. (n.d.-b). *Sahasrara Chakra*. Www.yogaindailylife.org. Retrieved January 7, 2023, from https://www.yogaindailylife.org/system/en/chakras/sahasrara-chakra

Yogi Cameron. (2009a, August 30). *An Introduction To The Root Chakra + How To Heal It*. Mindbodygreen. https://www.mindbodygreen.com/0-94/Root-Chakra-Healing-for-Beginners.html

Yogi Cameron. (2009b, August 30). *An Introduction To The Sacral Chakra + How To Heal It*. Mindbodygreen.

https://www.mindbodygreen.com/0-95/Sacral-Chakra-Healing-For-Beginners.html

Yogi Cameron. (2009c, August 30). *An Introduction To The Solar Plexus Chakra + How To Heal It.* Mindbodygreen. https://www.mindbodygreen.com/0-96/Solar-Plexus-Chakra-Healing-For-Beginners.html

Yogi Cameron. (2021, October 29). *mindbodygreen.* Mindbodygreen. https://www.mindbodygreen.com/0-91/The-7-Chakras-for-Beginners.html

Printed in Great Britain
by Amazon

36976315R00089